P9-DED-638

Combat Uniforms of the Civil War

Dedication of Monument
on Bull Run Battlefield,
photographed in 1865.

Combat Uniforms of the Civil War

Volume Two
The Federal Army

By Mark Lloyd
Illustrated by Mike Codd

Chelsea House Publishers
Philadelphia

Published in 1999 by
Chelsea House Publishers
1974 Sproul Road, Suite 400
P.O. Box 914
Broomall, PA19008-0914

Printed in China

Library of Congress Cataloging-in-Publication Data

Lloyd, Mark 1948-
Combat uniforms of the Civil War / Mark Lloyd: Illustrated by Mike Codd.
p. cm.
Includes index.
Summary: Describes the military uniforms worn by individual units of Federal and Confederate armies during the Civil War as well as the battlefield activities of these units.
1. United States. Army—Uniforms—Juvenile literature. 2. Confederate States of America. Army—Uniforms—Juvenile literature. 3. United States—History—Civil War, 1861-1865—Juvenile literature. [1. Military uniforms. 2. United States. Army. 3. Confederate States of America. Army. 4. United States—History—Civil War, 1861-1865.] I. Codd, Michael, ill. II. Title.
UC483.L55 1998
355. 1'4'0973—dc21 98-18187
CIP
AC

ISBN 0-7910-4993-0 (vol. 1)
ISBN 0-7910-4994-9 (vol. 2)
ISBN 0-7910-4995-7 (vol. 3)
ISBN 0-7910-4996-5 (vol. 4)
ISBN 0-7910-4992-2 (set)

Contents

U.S. Marine Corps	6
U.S. Army Hospital Steward	10
The Indiana Regiments	14
U.S. Military Railroad Engineers	18
Union Army Staff Officers	22
Trooper: U.S. Volunteer Cavalry	26
The Pennsylvania Reserves	30
Gunner: Heavy Artillery	34
U.S. Signal Corps	38
The Iron Brigade of the West	42
Support Troops	46
The Prisoner of War	50
Main Campaigns of the Civil War	54
Railroads of the Confederate and Border States	56
Map: First Battle of Bull Run (Manassas)	58
Map: Battle of Gettysburg	59
Index	60

A Company of Infantry, near Harper's Ferry.

U.S. MARINE CORPS

Despite its long and proud history, the U.S. Marine Corps remained relatively small throughout the Civil War. At no time did it number more than 4,167 officers and men, of whom 148 were killed in action. The Corps was too lightly armed and equipped to take a major part in the land war. It did, however, see action at the 1st Battle of Manassas (Bull Run) on 21 July 1861, and fought with conspicuous gallantry in the successful siege of Fort Fisher (6–15 January 1865). More conventionally, detachments served with all but the smallest ships, frequently giving a good account of themselves in the numerous bloody naval engagements of the war.

The prime task of the Union navy, and therefore of the Marines, was blockade. From the outset, General Winfield Scott, Lincoln's chief military adviser, realizing that the war would not be won within the enlistment period of the first 90-day volunteers, advocated the "Anaconda Plan" or constriction of the South. In essence, the navy would blockade the coast from the Potomac to New Orleans while the Army advanced down the Mississippi to the Gulf of Mexico. The Confederacy would then be split in two, with the populous areas of the east denied the foodstocks of the west, and would be forced into submission.

However, most obvious plans have their weaknesses and "Anaconda" was no exception. Many of the South's merchantmen had been deliberately constructed with shallow drafts and were therefore able to operate from small ports and inlets inaccessible to more conventional warships. More fundamentally, at the outbreak of hostilities the North had virtually no blockade ships available, a problem compounded by the highly successful Confederate raid on Norfolk. Initially, the four blockading squadrons – the North Atlantic under Goldsborough, the South Atlantic under DuPont, the East Gulf under McKean, and the West Gulf under Farragut – were simply too weak to carry out their duties effectively. By mid-summer, however, the Federal fleet had grown sufficiently to enable it to take the initiative. In August 1861, two Confederate forts at Hatteras Inlet on the North Carolina coast were stormed and captured, and in November Port Royal, strategically positioned on the South Carolina coast between Charleston and Savannah, was attacked. Plans to mount a joint army–navy

The dress uniform with its dark blue frock coat, yellow braid and scarlet trim, although impressive, was discarded as impractical during active campaigning.

Headdress: A *chasseur*-pattern field cap with an infantry horn cap badge containing the letter "M" in its center was issued to all but the hybrid Mississippi Marine Brigade.

Jacket: Blue frock coats with plain high collars were worn by N.C.O.s and Marines ashore. N.C.O.s wore gold chevrons with red edging. At sea these were often discarded in favor of a blue pullover shirt.

Weapons: Generally Marines were too lightly equipped to fight successfully ashore, although they did take part in one or two major battles.

assault were frustrated when the transports carrying the landing craft were driven ashore in a storm. Unperturbed, DuPont determined to attempt an unsupported naval attack relying on the Marines under his command for limited military assistance. On 7 November, DuPont attacked and overwhelmed the hastily constructed earthen forts at Fort Walker and Fort Beauregard. In so doing, he secured the outer Port Royal Sound, denying the enemy future use of the port. General Lee at once withdrew inland, allowing the Union to consolidate its hold on the coastal islands.

Port Royal was merely the first of a long series of Union victories along the South Atlantic coast and in the Gulf of Mexico. By 1864, only Charleston, South Carolina and Wilmington, North Carolina, on the Atlantic seaboard, remained open to Confederate blockade runners.

Spurred on by the success of DuPont in the Carolinas U.S. Navy Flag Officer David Farragut, commander of the West Gulf Squadron, planned an assault on the Confederate stronghold of New Orleans. The key Confederate defenses consisted of Forts Jackson and St. Philip situated astride the Mississippi at Plaquemine Bend some 90 miles by river from the city itself. In addition, a boom of logs linked by heavy chains barred the way. Eager to enhance the navy's prestige, Assistant Secretary of the Navy Gustavus Fox vetoed initial plans for a joint operation with the army and instead ordered a fleet of mortar boats under the command of Commander Porter to pound the forts into submission while Farragut's warships fought their way upriver. Porter's mortar boats began their bombardment on 17 April 1862, and a week later, Farragut's steam sloops forced their way through a break in the log boom. Unwilling to wait for a change of heart by the army and wishing to avail himself of the spring tide, Farragut immediately proceeded upriver to accept the surrender of New Orleans on 25 April. Yet again, the Federal navy, devoid of formal military help, had utilized its Marine contingent to the full to inflict a crippling blow on the enemy.

Not all unsupported naval actions were as successful. Soon after taking New Orleans, Farragut sailed with his fleet to Vicksburg. Although only a brigade defended the partially completed works, the Confederates refused to surrender. Farragut began a bombardment with his cruisers and gunboats, supported after 20 June by the newly arrived mortars, but to no avail. The siege was abandoned on 26 July when the navy, disillusioned by its first setback, returned to New Orleans and the Gulf.

The greatest single engagement of the war to involve the U.S. Marines was the dual between the ironclads *Virginia* and *Monitor* fought in Hampton Roads, Virginia on 9 March 1862. In their panic to

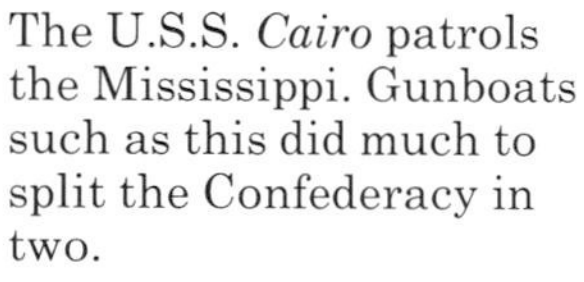

The U.S.S. *Cairo* patrols the Mississippi. Gunboats such as this did much to split the Confederacy in two.

Dress regulations at sea were usually relaxed. The presence of several black ratings bears witness to the U.S. Navy's policy of total integration.

evacuate Norfolk, the Union troops had failed to destroy completely the unseaworthy steam frigate *Merrimac*. The Confederates raised it, repaired it, coaxing life back into its damaged engines, armor-plated it and rechristened it *Virginia*. On 8 March, it steamed slowly but purposefully out of Norfolk harbor in search of the Federal flotilla. The *Cumberland* was rammed, the *Congress* sunk by gunfire, and a third major unit forced aground. By the sheerest of coincidences, as the *Virginia* returned triumphantly to her berth, the unsuspecting *Monitor* entered the far end of the sound. Designed by John Ericsson, an ex-patriate Swede, specifically to counter the ironclad threat, the *Monitor* was unique. Little more than an enormous raft, her superstructure, most of which was permanently below the waterline, was dominated by a single, huge, circular turret 20 ft (6m) in diameter and protected by 8-inch (20cm) iron plates. Firepower was provided by two 11-inch (28cm) Dahlgren smoothbore cannons, the mightiest conventional guns then at sea, manned by mixed crews of sailors and Marines. On 9 March, the two heavyweights joined ponderous battle. Neither was able to penetrate the armor of the other nor was the *Virginia* able to ram her adversary (she had, in any case, lost her ram when attacking *Cumberland* on the previous day). After four hours, dented and out of ammunition, the two giants disengaged, never to meet again.

Despite the relatively small size of the Marine Corps, its members enjoyed a wide variety of individual uniforms. Dress uniform was particularly impressive. The dark blue frock coat with its yellow braid and scarlet trim was embellished with gold or yellow worsted cuff lace to indicate rank. Field officers wore four gold lace loops, sergeant majors and quartermasters four of brass. Captains and sergeants wore three loops of gold and brass respectively, lieutenants and privates two. All ranks wore epaulettes on each shoulder, the width of the fringe indicating the rank. In addition, N.C.O.s wore gold chevrons edged with red. With the exception of staff officers who wore red, all ranks wore sky blue trousers embellished with a scarlet welt for officers and a scarlet stripe for senior N.C.O.s.

With the exception of the Mississippi Marine Brigade, created in November 1862 and comprising soldiers attached to the Mississippi fleet, which was therefore not a true Marine unit, all Marines wore a cap badge consisting of a gold wreath around a shield bearing an infantry horn with the Old English letter "M" within its loop.

For field purposes, all ranks wore dark blue frock coats with plain collars, although at sea enlisted men might wear a blue pullover-shirt over a white cotton shirt in preference. A dark blue "*chasseur*"-pattern field cap decorated with the infantry horn and the letter "M" was worn at all times. Inevitably, as equipment wore out, it was replaced with anything available, and as the war continued it was often difficult to differentiate between the Marines and the sailors with whom they lived and worked.

U.S. ARMY HOSPITAL STEWARD

Federal losses in the Civil War were horrific. Although exact figures are unavailable, an estimated 360,000 officers and men lost their lives. Of these, 110,000 – less than one-third of the total – were killed in action or mortally wounded. Of the remainder, a staggering 200,000 succumbed to disease, 25,000 died as prisoners of war, 10,000 were killed in accidents and 16,000 died from other causes. It has been suggested that a further 500,000 sustained non-fatal injuries, in many instances amputations. However, before hostilities began, no one could have anticipated the effect of modern weaponry on troops governed by the traditional tactic of the frontal assault.

At the outbreak of war, the U.S. Army Medical Department mustered a mere 115 officers and men, 27 of whom immediately resigned, all but three going to the South to form the embryonic Confederate Medical Department. As the war progressed, the Federal department grew in size and complexity until eventually it was led by a surgeon-general aided by an assistant surgeon-general. At its peak, it consisted of an inspector-general with 16 medical inspectors, 170 surgeons and assistants, 547 volunteer surgeons and assistant surgeons, 2,109 regimental surgeons, 3,882 regimental assistant surgeons, 85 acting staff surgeons and 5,532 acting assistant surgeons.

Surgeons were nominally commissioned as majors and assistant surgeons as captains. Both wore conventional staff uniforms with the added embellishments of a thin gold cord down each leg, medium or emerald green silk sashes and the letters "MS" interwoven in silver and gold into the epaulettes. In line with all staff officers, surgeons were permitted by an order of 22 November 1864 to remove their conspicuous epaulettes to make themselves less susceptible to sniper fire.

It was accepted that the professional surgeons could not hope to cater for the medical needs of tens of thousands of volunteers swelling the ranks of the army nor could they be expected to deal adequately with the huge numbers of injuries sustained in battle. At Chickamauga, for instance, an alleged 11,243 Federal troops, (20 percent of the combatants) were killed or injured, while at Antietam (Sharpsburg) – "the bloodiest one-day battle of the entire war" – a staggering 12,400 casualties were reported. Lengthy campaigns produced even greater carnage: in four weeks of bitter fighting in May and June 1864, encompassing the battles of Cold Harbor and Spotsylvania and the Wilderness campaign, treatment was given to 54,929 casualties, 52 percent of the Federal participants.

In an attempt to mitigate the resultant crisis, contract surgeons were occasionally hired, and

The evacuation of the wounded after the Battle of Seven Pines stretched Federal resources to the limit.

Frock coat: Stewards did not wear badges of rank on their otherwise traditional three-quarter length frock coats. Instead they wore a half-chevron of emerald green cloth with yellow edging bearing a badge of a yellow caduceus. A red worsted sash and broad crimson stripe along either seam of the trousers completed the specialist attire.

Knapsack: Wooden medical knapsacks containing medicines and a few crude surgical instruments were issued in 1862 and carried into the field by the stewards to ensure that the surgeons had supplies immediately to hand.

medical cadets (young men currently undertaking medical training) were enlisted. The contractees, jealous of their civilian status, retained their own clothes and were generally loath to operate beyond the relative protection of the large base hospitals. Even so, many, if unfortunately not all, performed excellent feats of surgery. Because of their youth and lack of experience, the cadets were often deployed further forward, assisting in the hospitals or dressing wounds in the field as circumstances required. Issued with the uniform of a second lieutenant, save for a forage cap in lieu of the less practical dress hat, and instantly recognizable by their green shoulder bars with a $\frac{1}{2}$-inch (1.3cm) gold strip running through the center, cadets unfortunate enough to be allocated to an active area of the front line must have offered tempting targets to the omnipresent enemy snipers. Details of their losses are, however, not recorded.

Many of the mundane duties at regimental level were delegated to the hospital steward – a senior non-commissioned officer tasked to assist the surgeon when and where required. Realistically, the steward's work must have brought him hourly into contact with the carnage of the operating table and the pandemonium of the make-shift post-operative wards, yet his official dress remained the somewhat impractical frock coat. A "half-chevron" of emerald green cloth with yellow edging bearing a badge of a yellow caduceus was worn on the upper sleeve as a badge of rank. Other embellishments consisted of a mixed green-and-buff cord around the otherwise conventional "Hardee" hat, a red worsted sash, and a broad crimson stripe along the outer seam of the trousers.

Medical staff at the front fought a constant and largely unsuccessful battle against disease. Lack of discipline and apathy combined with ignorance to make the military encampments hot beds of typhoid, smallpox, and other ailments usually associated with overcrowding and lack of sanitation. Regular units – and, notably, as the war progressed, black troops – invariably maintained at least minimum standards of hygiene. However, many of the younger volunteers shunned as unnecessarily regimental the washing and changing of clothes, with inevitable results.

As the war continued and numbers became critical, field commanders became increasingly uneasy at the high incidence of illness and disease within the ranks and at last began to heed the advice of their medical staffs. Discipline was tightened, the rudiments of hygiene enforced, and parades increased.

Conditions in the front-line trenches could not always be controlled. General Andrew Humphreys, then Meade's chief of staff and an accomplished engineer, reported plaintively after the Battle of Cold Harbor that, during the campaign, his troops had been forced to seek shelter in waterlogged trenches with little food and only tainted water to drink. The surrounding land was low, flat, and covered with the decaying bodies of the dead. Not surprisingly, malaria was rife.

Within 20 minutes of the storming of Marye's Heights, the wounded had been taken to regimental aid posts, leaving the dead alone, awaiting burial.

Evacuation of the non-walking wounded from the battlefield to the first aid dressing station was chaotic. Bandsmen were given the duty of stretcher bearers but were too few in number to carry out the task adequately. Their ranks were swelled by sections of ten men per regiment assigned to render assistance, but it soon became clear that the commanders were taking the opportunity of divesting themselves of their very worst men for this task. The wounded were often left for hours, and sometimes days, without help. Truces for the collection of the wounded from the battlefield were rare, and reports of men crying out in agony from no man's land for the want of water and shelter were common.

A few generals, notably Sherman, attempted as far as possible to retain the wounded at regimental level where they considered that care would be of a higher, more personal standard. However, an unfortunate parochialism ensued in which surgeons tended to ignore seriously injured men of other units to concentrate on the members of their own. Divisional hospitals – clusters of between 20 and 30 tents deemed sufficient to cope with the medical needs of 8,000 fighting men – were gradually established in the rear areas safe from enemy artillery fire. Eventually the regimental posts were disbanded, their staffs being assimilated into the less partisan divisional structure.

Initially, evacuation of the wounded was the responsibility of the Quartermaster Corps. However, numerous complaints that many drivers were simply refusing to enter the battle zone, compounded by several instances of horses being commandeered to pull guns or furnish remounts for the cavalry, led in August 1862 to the creation within the Army of the Potomac of an independent Federal Ambulance Corps. The standard ambulance, the so-called "rocker" type, was a four-wheeled vehicle pulled by two horses and manned by a driver and two stretcher bearers. As far as possible, each ambulance was self-contained, with a supply of fresh drinking water, cans of beef stock, bread and cooking apparatus carried on each vehicle. Three ambulances, under the overall command of a sergeant, were attached to each regiment. Brigade ambulances were the responsibility of a second lieutenant and, from 1864 onwards, divisional vehicles were under the charge of a full lieutenant. At first, Ambulance Corps troops wore caps with green bands 2 inches (5cm) broad around them and a green half-chevron above the elbow on each arm. All were armed with revolvers for self-defense. As the war progressed, the chevrons were reduced in size, and each command adopted the practice of designating its men with individual field insignia.

The most seriously injured soldiers were evacuated to huge permanent base hospitals. Transportation was invariably by train although, when convenient, ships were occasionally pressed into service. Hospital trains at first consisted of no more than a collection of empty boxcars provided with straw on which to lay the litters, but as time passed, conditions gradually improved. Conventional passenger rolling stock was gutted and refitted with bunks, while special cars were transformed into dispensaries and emergency operating rooms.

Civilians – and, in the latter stages of the war, an increasingly large number of women – were employed in the base hospitals to augment the meager military resources. Never popular with the conservatives, the women nevertheless played a vital role, adding a degree of compassion to an otherwise cold and frightening environment.

The wounded gather at a field hospital after the Battle of Fredericksburg.

An ambulance train photographed in July 1863, en route to Harewood Hospital.

THE INDIANA REGIMENTS

At the outbreak of war, there were only six volunteer companies active in the entire state of Indiana. However, within a few weeks no fewer than six regiments of volunteers had flocked to the colors. Most joined initially for three months, but when it became apparent that this would be totally inadequate for the task ahead, they willingly re-enlisted for three years. Initially, the majority of troops were issued with a gray uniform dangerously similar at a distance to that of the Confederacy. The senior regiments, designated the 6th and 7th in deference to the 1st to 5th Regiments which had fought honorably in the earlier Mexican War, wore short gray padded jackets and gray trousers with blue flannel shirts, the 8th short light blue jackets and trousers, the 9th gray satinet jackets and trousers, and the 10th light blue jean jackets and trousers.

Under the patronage of its colonel-in-chief, Lew Wallace, previously the Governor of New Mexico and later author of *Ben Hur*, the 11th Indiana Regiment adopted the more picturesque if far less practical uniform of the North African Zouaves. Wallace, however, ensured that, unlike some of the ridiculously over-dressed Eastern Zouave regiments, the 11th never became a laughing stock. In his own words:

> There was nothing of the flashy, Algerian colors in the uniform, no red fez, no red breeches, no red or yellow sash with tassels big as early cabbages. Our outfit was of the tamest gray, twilled goods, not unlike home-made jeans, and a vizor cap, French in pattern, its top of red cloth not larger than the palm of one's hand; a blue flannel shirt with open neck; a jacket Greekskin form, edges with narrow binding, breeches baggy, but not pettycoated; button gaiters connecting below the knee with the breeches and strapped over the shoe.

Major General Thomas Meagher, photographed here proudly wearing the "Hardee" hat of the Iron Brigade of the West.

Despite their popularity with the men, the early uniforms of the various Indiana Regiments did not find favor with government officials in Washington who wrote to Governor Morton respectfully requesting that no further regiments be dressed in gray, "that being the color generally worn by the enemy." As a result, regiments raised subsequently wore standard Federal issue U.S. Army uniforms. However, many were issued with blue fatigue jackets similar in design to the original gray apparel, and with distinctive broad-brimmed black hats subsequently adopted by the Iron Brigade of the West in which the 19th Indiana was destined to play a prominent role.

Ever conscious of the need for practicality yet unwilling to allow the 11th to lose its identity completely, Wallace came up with a new uniform for his Zouaves in December 1861. A black Zouave-style jacket was introduced as were sky blue regulation uniform trousers and a dark blue uniform cap. A dark blue woolen vest was worn as an undergarment beneath the jacket. Surprisingly, the original red-topped fatigue caps, ideal targets for enemy snipers, continued to be worn instead of the blue fatigue caps, which were never issued.

In common with many regiments of the time, the majority of Indiana Volunteer N.C.O.s did not carry the impractical sword. They replaced it with a leather cartridge box worn on the belt to the right of the buckle.

Initially the state's early regiments were issued with the Model 1842 musket. Later, however, Indiana purchased 40,000 far superior P1853 Enfield rifled muskets with which it armed approximately half of its volunteers, equipping the rest with a modern mixture of domestically produced weapons, notably the M1855 "Harpers Ferry" rifle with its fiercesome sword bayonet.

In accordance with Federal military thinking, the Indiana regiments were not brigaded together but instead served independently under a number of commands. The 19th Indiana was arguably the most famous. Organized in Indianapolis on 29 July 1861, it arrived in Washington on 5 August to join the army then forming for an attack south into Virginia. Commanded at various times by Solomon Meredith, Samuel Williams, and John Lindley, it served throughout much of its existence as part of the Iron Brigade of the West. It first saw service at Lewinsville, Virginia (11 September 1861) as part of the Army of the Potomac, and subsequently fought at the 2nd Battle of Manassas (Bull Run), losing 259 out of 423 engaged, at South Mountain where it sustained 53 casualties, and at Antietam (Sharpsburg) where it lost a further 72 officers and

Headdress: The wide-brimmed light-blue hats initially issued to the regiment were ultimately replaced by darker "Hardee" hats later to become the hallmark of the "Iron Brigade of the West."

Jacket: With the exception of the 11th Indianas who wore Zouave-style jackets and trousers, the regiment was issued with gray uniforms trimmed with black. Despite representations from Washington, these remained popular at grass roots level until the end of the war. The more realistic, however, changed to blue.

Weapons: Initially troops were issued with M1842 muskets. Later approximately half received the much improved British P1853 Enfield rifled musket.

men from the remaining 200 combatants. In 1863, the bloody Battle of Gettysburg cost it a staggering 210 killed, injured and missing out of a total of 288 engaged, while in the fighting from the Wilderness to Petersburg (5 May – 30 July 1864), a further 226 fell. Major Isaac May was killed at the head of his men at the 2nd Manassas, Lieutenant Colonel Alois Bachman died at Antietam, and, most tragically of all, Colonel Williams was killed at the Wilderness.

Many of the newer volunteer regiments, although lacking the prestige of the older units and the *elan* of the Iron Brigade, nevertheless fought bravely and well throughout their engagement. Under the command initially of Colonel William Brown and subsequently of Colonels John Wheeler, William Taylor and William Orr, the 20th Indiana served with distinction from its inception in July 1861 to Appomattox and the final victory. Tasked in the early stages with the uninspiring duty of guarding the railroad near Cockeysville, Maryland, north of Baltimore, against Confederate sympathizers and raiding parties, the regiment was moved on 24 September to Hatteras Inlet, North Carolina, and then to Fort Monroe, Virginia for the winter. While there, it witnessed the *Monitor-Merrimac* (*Virginia*) engagement (see p. 58), lining the banks to protect the disabled *Congress* from capture, but otherwise saw no direct action. Sent to reinforce McClellan's army on the Peninsula, the regiment was assigned to Brigadier Robinson's 1st Brigade, itself part of Major General Kearney's 3rd Division, III Corps. On 25 June 1862, while forming part of the army's left flank, the regiment experienced its first major fight, sustaining 125 casualties when the

The Indiana Regiment played a key role in the capture of Fort Donelson.

The 1855-pattern Harpers Ferry musket was produced in large numbers throughout the war.

Confederates attacked in strength in the "Orchards" area. The regiment was again heavily engaged at Glendale, suffering ten fatalities, and at 2nd Manassas when a further 45, including Colonel Brown, were killed.

Due to its heavy losses, III Corps was withdrawn from the front immediately prior to Antietam and assigned to the defenses of Washington. From there, the 20th Indiana marched northwest to Gettysburg where, as part of Ward's Brigade, Birney's Division, it lost 156 all ranks, including Colonel Wheeler, in the ensuing battle. In 1864, during the final stages of the war, the regiment was transferred to II Corps where it sustained further heavy casualties in the Wilderness (33 killed), at Spotsylvania (18 killed), and at the siege of Petersburg, during which it suffered a further 22 fatalities including Lieutenant Colonel Meikel.

Under the inspired leadership of Colonel Silas Colgrove, the 27th Indiana left the state on 15 September 1861 to join Banks' command in Washington. As part of Gordon's 3rd Brigade, Williams' 1st Division, it first saw action in Jackson's campaign in the Shenandoah Valley in the summer of 1862. Assigned with the rest of the division to the newly formed XII Corps in September 1862, it fought with distinction at Cedar Mountain, losing 50 casualties, and at Antietam where it lost a further 209. In the thick of the fighting at Chancellorsville and at Gettysburg, where it suffered 150 and 110 dead and wounded respectively, the regiment constantly refused to yield ground, maintaining at all times the highest standards of morale. Uniquely, throughout its three years of service, while many units around it were all but disintegrating, the 27th lost only one man to desertion. As the war drew to a close, the regiment was posted to the West where, during its final formal engagement at Resaca, Georgia (13–16 May 1864), it was credited not only with capturing the colors and the colonel of the 38th Alabama Regiment but with inflicting five times its own casualties on the enemy. At a time when many regiments were beginning to scent victory and not unnaturally were demonstrating a marked reluctance to fight, the 27th continued to epitomize the fighting qualities of the Indiana volunteers as a whole by refusing to compromise the high standards which had made them so respected a part of the Union cause.

U.S. MILITARY RAILROAD ENGINEERS

The military potential of the railroads had been exploited by several European powers well before the onset of the American Civil War. As early as 1830, the British War Office had experimented with moving troops by rail, and in 1842, Prussia had begun actively to consider the feasibility of constructing new lines which, while serving the day-to-day needs of the civilian population, would allow the rapid movement of troops from its eastern to its western borders or vice versa should both be threatened simultaneously. Within three years, tracks had been laid to both frontiers, and in 1846, the Prussian army moved 12,000 men from Potsdam, its headquarters on the outskirts of Berlin, east to Posen (now the Polish city of Poznán) in record time.

The first recorded use of railroads in war came in 1859 when France invaded Italy in response to a request for help from the Vatican. Within the space of 86 days, the French had moved 600,000 men and 129,000 horses to the border. Such efficiency, however, brought with it its own problems: large numbers of men and horses were deposited in isolated areas at railheads where they were forced to wait, hungry and militarily impotent, while their rations, ammunition, and other supplies were brought up by conventional mule train.

At the outbreak of the Civil War, there were approximately 22,000 miles of track in the North compared with 9,000 miles in the Confederacy. At its best, Union track was excellent, far better than that in the South, but at its worst, it was wholly inadequate for the task ahead. Sleepers were generally laid straight on bare earth without any stone or gravel ballast; gradients were avoided as far as possible to minimize the strain on the under-powered locomotives; and lines were routed around hills to avoid the expense of constructing the cuttings and tunnels which would otherwise have been needed to keep the gradients below an acceptable minimum.

Due to the poor track, the large number of sharp bends caused by the rerouting around natural obstacles, and the relatively low power of the engines, few trains exceeded 25mph or pulled weights exceeding 150 tons. The lines themselves were owned by a multitude of small but fiercely competitive companies, few of whom had reached any form of commercial agreement with their rivals. Gages varied considerably, and each company operated its own depots, making uninterrupted long-distance travel all but impossible. Depots were often miles apart, necessitating the time-consuming transfer of passengers and freight by wagon before a journey might be continued.

Many Northern lines were too far to the north or west to become involved tactically; they simply carried on as before, growing rich on the increased

Heavy mortars were occasionally mounted on reinforced railroad trolleys and fired into the enemy's defensive positions from specially constructed tracks. Recoil was a constant problem.

Although strenuous attempts were made to bring the railroads, particularly those in the west, under Federal control, the majority of engineers remained civilian. Few if any wore uniform. Weapons were carried primarily for personal protection or to settle feuds. However the Confederate cavalry made frequent sorties against Federal lines of communication and danger was therefore never far away.

volume of traffic. Those closer to the battlefront became more directly a part of the war. Occasionally this led to a conflict of interests for the railroad directors – never more so than in 1861 when the president of the Baltimore & Ohio was threatened with both the confiscation by the Confederacy of his company's track laid within the jurisdiction of the Confederate state of Virginia if he carried Federal troops, and with an indictment for treason from the U.S. Secretary of the Interior if he refused.

Within days of the attack on Fort Sumter, Lincoln created the United States Military Railway Service with notional powers of seizure over all Northern lines. At first, very little was done to implement these powers, and the various companies were left to handle military traffic as if it were civilian. However, as the war progressed and the army swelled from under 20,000 to nearly 2 million men, the existing system with its multitude of owners and operating procedures, its plethora of gages, and, above all, its petty rivalries began to prove wholly inadequate. In August 1861, Thomas Scott, vice president of the Pennsylvania Railroad, was made Assistant Secretary of War with special responsibility for the military control of railroads. His first act was to appoint Daniel Craig McCallum, then the general secretary of the Erie Railroad, as military director and superintendent of military railroads in the West. A lively Scot and brilliant engineer, McCallum immediately set about the consolidation of the tracks under his authority, adding many miles to their existing lengths.

Shortly afterward Herman Haupt, a civil engineer and lecturer in mathematics at Penn College near Gettysburg, was appointed to a similar post in the East. Haupt's first task was to rebuild the elements of the Richmond, Fredericksburg & Potomac Railroad which had been comprehensively destroyed by the Confederates during their retreat before the advance of McDowell's troops on Richmond. The Union had been relying on the track for the transportation of all its supplies, and Haupt had the formidable task of assembling a construction force, gathering raw material, and repairing the line, all of which he completed in a record three weeks – a feat made all the more remarkable when it is realized that his duties included the rebuilding of a wooden bridge 400 ft (122m) long and 100 ft (30m) above the Potomac. Haupt was promoted to brigadier general in September 1862 but resigned less than a year later, expressing a willingness to continue without official rank or pay as long as no restrictions were placed on his work. Freed of government bureaucracy, he continued to serve the Union faithfully for the rest of the war.

Initially, the Confederacy utilized its limited rail resources far more successfully than the Union. Prior to the 1st Battle of Manassas (Bull Run), Jackson's entire brigade was moved by rail to Manassas Junction, allowing it to take up a strategic position ahead of the advancing Federals. (Ironically it would have been joined by Bartow's brigade of Georgians had the railroad workers not refused to work the overtime necessary to make a second trip). Lee made excellent use of the railroads during the Seven Days campaign in defense of Richmond in June/July 1862 and again in the recapture of Knoxville in September 1863.

Attempts by the Union to move its far larger

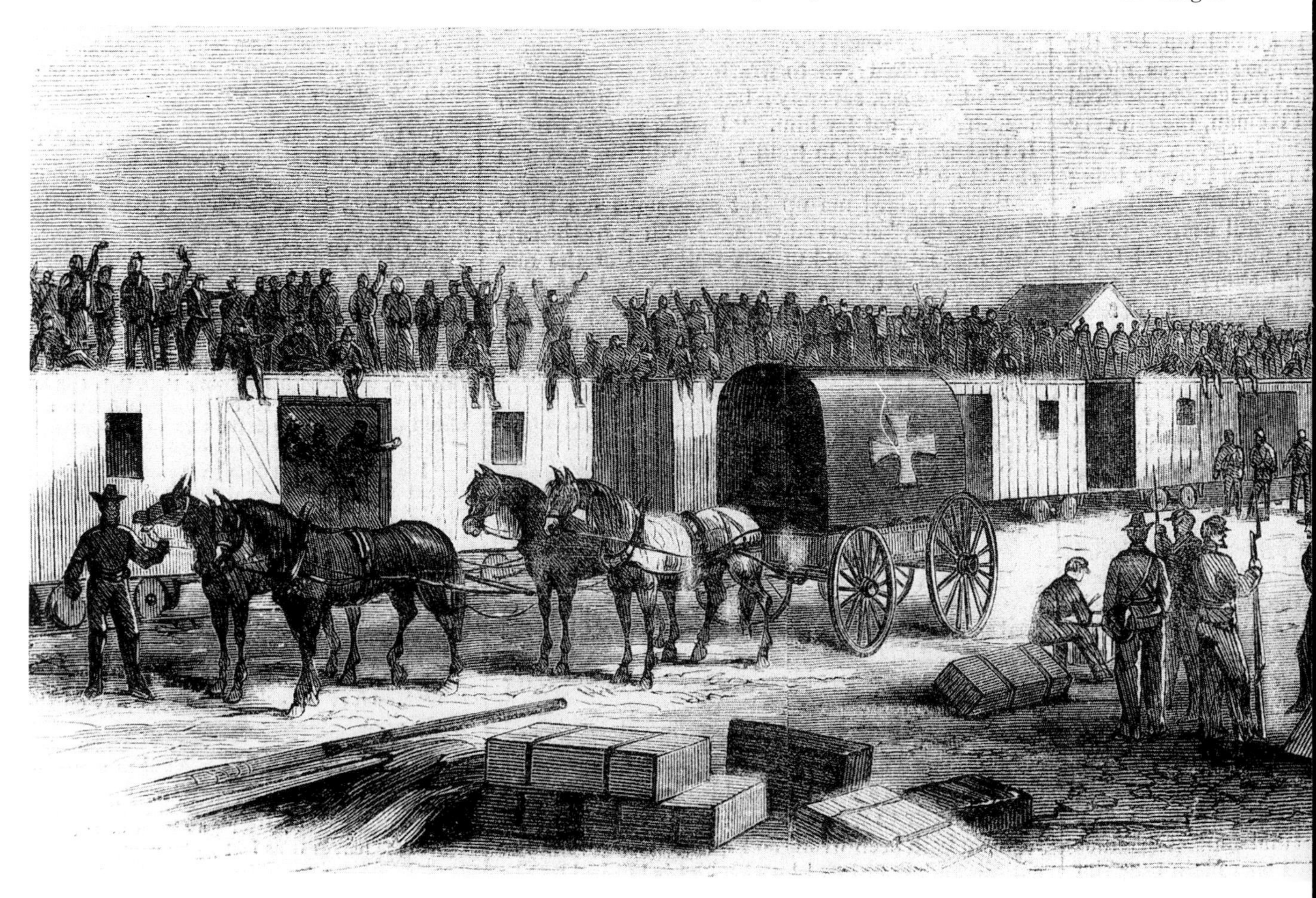

Federal reinforcements arriving by train during the battle at Peebles' Farm, September 1864. Acute overcrowding of rolling stock led to numerous derailments.

Herman Haupt in his personal locomotive, from which he supervised the construction gangs. He is standing on the footplate, by the circular window.

numbers of troops the considerable distances required were often frustrated by the railroad's total inability to cope. When Grant attempted to relieve Rosecrans' beleaguered troops in Chattanooga in October 1863, he found the Nashville & Chattanooga Railroad sadly lacking. In poor condition, inefficiently administered, and hazardous, its single track was simply incapable of moving the minimum of 30 supply trucks required daily to sustain the defenders. Eventually three existing one-track railroads – the Nashville & Chattanooga, the Memphis & Charleston, and the Nashville & Decatur – were linked to form a 200-mile one-way circuit which proved just sufficient for the task. Even this could not operate until an entire infantry division had been allocated the task of repairing the southern perimeter of the arc, including no fewer than 18 bridges destroyed by raiding Confederate cavalry.

Sherman's famous "march to the sea" in December 1864 depended heavily on the railroad for the maintenance of its supply line which, toward the end of the campaign, stretched for over 450 miles. Divided into three sectors – Louisville–Nashville (185 miles), Nashville–Chattanooga (151 miles), and, eventually, Chattanooga–Atlanta (137 miles) – the track was constantly liable to attack by Confederate raiding parties and, forward from Chattanooga, had to be closely guarded by Federal troops who were badly needed elsewhere. Once the track was built as far as Chattanooga, finding sufficient locomotives and rolling stock proved a logistical nightmare. Sherman requisitioned every locomotive entering Nashville but even these were not enough, and it was only when engines were brought from the far north, civilian travel was banned, and movement of any kind was limited to the transport of essential food, ammunition, and equipment that supply at last outstripped demand.

The operation of the railroads was greatly facilitated by the growth in the use of the electric telegraph and the introduction of Morse code. Every station was connected to the system and could be used to relay orders to trains, which would be picked up at the next depot. In this way, trains could be requisitioned from great distances and moved along alien track with relative ease. Above all, stretches of track could be kept clear once a train had entered them.

Despite the tremendous improvements which the railroad system underwent throughout the war, it was never completely capable of fulfilling the tasks allotted it. Whether this was due to the inherent reluctance of the majority of the proprietors to relinquish control of their companies to the State, or whether it was due to the total inability of the higher command to comprehend the virtual impossibility of blending literally hundreds of often tiny and mutually distrustful organizations into one homogeneous unit remains a moot point.

UNION ARMY STAFF OFFICERS

Not unnaturally, the miniscule pre-war staff which had ably served the peacetime army of 16,000 officers and men proved totally inadequate for the needs of the 2 million enlisted into war service. As a result, more soldiers were promoted to the rank of full general between 1861 and 1865 than had served in the entire Engineer Corps in 1860.

With the exception of army commanders, general officers were expected to lead from the front. Long supply lines were not encouraged nor was a reliance on second-hand information. Of the 583 officers appointed to the rank of general throughout the war, 47 were either killed in action or subsequently died of their wounds, a level of casualties unrivaled before or since.

Although regulations for the organization of staff and their duties did exist, these were largely ignored by many of the field commanders, who preferred to depend on the advice and assistance of a small nucleus of trusted personnel than on that of a large number of inexperienced and, on occasion, political appointees. When General Grant was promoted to the newly created rank of lieutenant general, he was authorized a personal staff of a brigadier general as chief-of-staff, four aides-de-camp with the rank of lieutenant colonel, and two lieutenant colonels as military secretaries. In the field, Grant supplemented these with two lieutenant colonels acting as assistant adjutant general and assistant inspector general, three staff captains, and two junior officers as A.D.C.s.

Unlike a modern headquarters, which differentiates totally between supply and administration, overall control of all aspects of staff work was

Brevet Major General Rufus Ingalls, U.S. Cavalry, photographed wearing the uniform of a brigadier.

Headdress: Most senior staff officers interpreted dress regulations loosely. Their black felt hats were meant to be 6.25-in tall with brims of 3.25-in worn pinned up on the right, but most wore them slouched for comfort. However the cap badge with its silver embroidered letters "US" inscribed in Old English within an embroidered wreath seems to have been universally worn.

Tunic: Theoretically major-generals wore double-breasted frock coats with nine buttons placed in threes in each of two rows while brigadiers had eight buttons in each row placed in pairs. In practice many commanders wore far simpler sack coats with buttons of their choosing. Regulation standing collars were usually abandoned as impractical.

General Blanker, at the head of his brigade, covering the retreat from Bull Run.

vested in the chief-of-staff. A.D.C.s were used to transmit orders direct from the commander to the troops on the ground with the result that, occasionally, intermediate commanders were circumvented. Inevitably this led to confusion, if not catastrophe. When in overall supreme command, Grant, a man renowned for direct action, frequently took personal control of elements of the Army of the Potomac, leaving its commanding general – the brilliant if irascible but fortunately loyal Meade – confused and impotent. Numerous attempts were made by Grant's staff to undermine Meade's status and position, but fortunately, although Grant listened attentively to their blatant disloyalty to a senior officer, he ignored their pleas for Meade's dismissal, allowing him to continue with at least the vestiges of authority.

General Andrew Humphreys, the chief-of-staff to General Meade and a highly competent and experienced regular officer, summed up the weaknesses of this dual command system when he later wrote of his experiences in Virginia:

> There were two officers commanding the same army. Such a mixed command was not calculated to produce the best results that either singly was capable of bringing about. It naturally caused some vagueness and uncertainty as to the exact sphere of each, and sometimes took away from the positiveness, fullness and earnestness of the consideration of an intended operation or tactical movement that, had there been but one commander, would have had the most earnest attention and corresponding action.

Left to his own devices in the West, Sherman was able to devolve a smaller, more intimate staff system. Doing away completely with the position of chief-of-staff, he ordered each of his regimental colonels to appoint a competent adjutant, a quartermaster, a commissary, and a team of three to four doctors to deal with the daily needs of each individual unit. Each brigade and divisional headquarters was given a similar team, the divisional HQ supplemented with a cadre of engineers. Unlike Grant who frequently interfered with the activities of his subordinates, Sherman accepted totally the need for delegation, granting his juniors immense power when necessary. In direct contrast to Meade, who admittedly was burdened with the execution of many of Grant's more mundane duties, Sherman's tactical headquarters typically consisted of no more than six wagons supported by a company of Ohio sharpshooters for protection and a company of Alabama irregular cavalry to provide orderlies and carry messages.

The greatest weakness in the Federal staff system lay in the fact that the quartermaster, commissary, and ordnance departments were all fiercely independent of the commander in the field, owing their allegiance direct to their masters in Washington. Although Grant complained bitterly of this anomaly, occasionally to Lincoln himself, nothing was done to subordinate these support units which remained independent throughout the war.

In the early stages of the conflict, staff officers, few of whom had any real military experience, were generally of a very low standard. Many commanders refused to commit their orders to writing, preferring to rely on verbal dissemination which frequently led to confusion – and occasionally on a gigantean scale. Exceptionally, Grant wrote out the majority of his orders and instructions himself, dispatching them via courier. Although this increased the possibility of compromise through loss or capture, it completely removed the fear of misunderstanding and added weight to orders which might otherwise have been ignored by independently minded subordinates.

Matters improved steadily as individuals gained in experience, so much so that the withdrawal of the Army of the Potomac from Cold Harbor across the James River in June 1864 is still regarded as one of the finest examples of staff planning and efficiency in the history of the United States army. Under the cover of darkness and in complete secrecy, the entire army disengaged and moved south, crossing the James River via a 2,100 ft (640m) long pontoon bridge constructed by Captain G.H. Mendell and 450 engineers in only eight hours. General Fuller described the entire exercise as "one of the finest operations of war ever carried out." Although this is certainly true, it must be remembered that had it not been for Lieutenant Colonels (later Generals) Comstock and Porter who, as Grant's A.D.C.s liaised with the subordinate commanders, reconnoitered the route, and planned the site for the bridge, so complicated a maneuver would almost certainly have ended in chaos.

The heavy losses among front line officers during the bloody fighting of 1863 and 1864 did much to undermine morale, particularly among the new recruits, many of whom were conscripts without the commitment of the earlier volunteers. Low morale often manifested itself in indiscipline, malingering, and desertion, which occasionally reached horrific proportions. Immediately after the Fredericksburg campaign (November–December 1862), desertions from the Army of the Potomac reached 200 per day, and at one stage, 85,123 men from that army alone had gone AWOL. There can be no doubt that an injection of good replacement officers into brigades and regiments which had suffered badly would have done much for morale, yet inexplicably Washington refused to sanction such a move. Instead, regiments which were too far below strength to function properly were reduced to battalion status and their surplus officers discharged or offered the possibility of a commission in a newly formed regiment. In the words of Sherman:

> If the worst enemy of the United States were to devise a plan to break down our army, a better one could not be attempted. Two years have been spent in educating colonels, captains, sergeants and corporals and now they are to be driven out of the service.

Standards of dress among general officers varied widely. Meade was a stickler for regulations, insisting that his officers wore regulation uniform although he occasionally allowed himself the luxury of an individualistic form of headdress. Grant, by contrast, regarded details of uniform as a tiresome irrelevancy and allowed his staff maximum personal discretion. Generals were issued with a double-breasted frock coat with a dark blue velvet collar and cuffs. Major generals wore twin rows of nine buttons in groups of threes, brigadier generals eight buttons in pairs. On formal occasions, a gold epaulette with silver stars (two for a major general and one for a brigadier) was worn on each shoulder. At other times, a black shoulder strap edged with gold embroidery and containing the same stars was substituted. The uniform was completed with a white shirt, black tie, dark blue waistcoat, plain dark blue trousers, and a black felt hat pinned up on the right side.

In the field, many senior officers wore dark blue variants of the civilian "sack coat" with turned-down blue collars and plain blue trousers. The hat was frequently "punched up" in the manner of a dunce's cap emphasizing the cap badge incorporating the Old English letters "US" within a gold embroidered wreath.

Some officers, notably Major General Warren, always maintained the highest personal standards in the presence of their men. Others, such as Burnside, dressed for comfort although rarely to the degree of Grant who frequently resembled an ill-kempt civilian rather than the supreme commander of the Union army.

Staff officers from the Adjutant General's, Inspector General's, Quartermaster and Pay departments wore the same basic uniform with plain blue collars and cuffs. Field-grade staff officers wore twin rows of seven buttons, junior officers one row. Epaulettes were marked with the wearer's corps insignia as well as his rank insignia.

Major General George G. Meade photographed with his staff officers.

TROOPER: U.S. VOLUNTEER CAVALRY

Prior to the outbreak of the war, the cavalry had played only the smallest part in the life and organization of the U.S. Army. It had none of the panache of the European hussars or lancers with their flamboyant uniforms and socially conscious officer corps, and lacked a sense of tradition both on and off the battlefield. Simplistically, the cavalry was regarded as an expensive irrelevancy by the military commanders of the day. Yet by Appomattox, the Union had brought into being no fewer than 258 cavalry regiments supported by a further 170 independent cavalry companies.

For the first two years of the war, the Union commanders demonstrated a marked lack of understanding of the potential of the massed mounted attack against raw infantry, preferring to commit the cavalry in small groups whenever and wherever they could be exploited in the short term. To compound the problem, individual cavalry units were frequently taken out of the line to act as escorts for convoys, guards for headquarters, military police, and even garrisons for captured enemy towns. However, by early 1864 it had at last been accepted that the Confederate use of cavalry *en masse* was far superior. Brigades and, later, divisions were formed and large scale maneuvers in all environments practiced. As the Union blockade of the South intensified, so the quality of the Confederate cavalry diminished, until by mid-1864, its indisputable superiority became a matter of history. The performance of cavalry is largely governed by the state of its mounts, and by the final winter of the war, Confederate horses were dying in large numbers from exhaustion compounded by malnutrition. Even so, by this stage the Union cavalry had improved so considerably that it is probable that its better units would have proved more than a match for the vaunted forces of Jeb Stuart at their height.

Prior to the war, the role of the cavalry had been seen almost exclusively as the suppression of the Indian nations in the far West. When Texas voted to secede on 1 February 1861 and the 1st U.S. Cavalry was forced to retire in haste to the safety of Kansas, a void was left in the sparsely populated areas of the Midwest. Acutely aware of the very real danger of an Indian uprising, Congress authorized the creation of a number of volunteer regiments to take the place of the hard corps of regulars whose presence was required urgently for the battles to come.

Few of the Northern states had a sufficient surplus of horsemen, let alone mounts, to raise whole regiments without considerable difficulty, and they therefore tended to concentrate on the creation of new infantry regiments to the detriment of the cavalry. Furthermore, whereas local dignitaries tended to regard it as their patriotic duty to raise, arm, equip, and even train units which would later bear their names, few if any seemed inclined to support the cavalry. Consequently, few troops were raised until the autumn of 1861, and of these, hardly any were capable of active service until the following summer. Fortunately for the settlers, the Indians failed to take advantage of this critical period, preferring to concentrate on survival through the bitter winter, and thus denied themselves their greatest opportunity in decades to strike a blow against a weakened and divided enemy.

An indication of the lack of natural horsemen in the Northern states can be gained from a comparison of the number of infantry and cavalry regiments raised. Indiana, for instance, raised 13 cavalry and 152 infantry regiments, Illinois 17

By 1865 the Horse Artillery and Cavalry had learned to work together as a single potent entity, capable of exploiting the many weaknesses in the rapidly dwindling Confederate lines.

Headdress: Many officers wore the plain McClellan hat with its thin pointed peak in preference to the heavier regulation issue.

Jacket: Although the frock coat remained official wear for officers, many preferred the short plain jacket. Some, as here, even wore their dress jacket devoid of all formal accoutrements save for one or two rows of buttons.

Weapons: Uniquely, until 1863 the 6th Pennsylvania Cavalry carried a European-style lance. An excellent weapon in the hands of shock troops trained to fight in the close confines of continental Europe, the lance proved quite useless in the open plains of the United States and was eventually discarded in favor of the more conventional saber, pistol and carbine.

cavalry and 156 infantry, Iowa 9 cavalry and 51 infantry, Missouri (a relatively rural state) 32 cavalry and 266 infantry, and New York 32 cavalry and 254 infantry.

As the war progressed, Federal armies in the West made increasing use of mounted infantry, frequently including them with cavalry regiments in cavalry brigades. Illinois and Indiana, in particular, provided a large number of mounted infantry, suggesting that neither state had made full initial use of its available horsemen. The 17th and 72nd Indiana Infantry Regiments, for example, were mounted in February and March 1863 respectively and both dismounted in November 1864, while the 9th and 92nd Illinois Infantry were both mounted in March 1863 and retained that status for the rest of the war.

Pennsylvania provided perhaps the most unusual cavalry unit. Rush's Lancers (6th Pennsylvania Cavalry) were armed with European-style lances, as well as pistols and the occasional carbine, until 1863 when they reverted to conventional weaponry.

Other unusual volunteer units were less successful. The 3rd New Jersey Cavalry – or "1st U.S. Hussars" as they preferred to be known – were quickly christened the "Butterflies" in response to the gaudiness of their uniforms, especially their heavily yellow-braided hussar jackets. Gentle mockery, however, turned to outright contempt when during a critical stage of the Battle of Yellow Tavern, six miles north of Richmond, on 11 May 1864, the entire unit retreated in disarray as soon as they came under enemy artillery fire. Suggestions by an embarrassed company commander that, the shells having stampeded the horses, the men had gone looking for them provoked an observer from the 7th Maine Infantry to exclaim in frustration, "We had many kinds of material in the Army of the

Officers and troopers of the 1st U.S. Cavalry rest after the Battle of Brandy Station during which, for the first time, they proved that the Confederate cavalry was not invincible.

Potomac and use for most of it, but not for the 'Uhlanen' (cavalry)."

More typical if less superficially impressive was the 1st Independent Battalion, Ohio Volunteer Cavalry. Raised in late 1861 and trained in Camp Dennison, Ohio, it was sent to Benton Barracks, Missouri in March 1862 and from there to Fort Laramie, Wyoming. Redesignated the 11th Ohio Volunteer Cavalry Regiment, the unit was subsequently split up between a number of posts including Fort Halleck, Sweetwater Station, and Fort Mitchell.

Throughout the war, over 20,000 volunteer cavalrymen were deployed in the West, although it was not until August 1862 that they were first called on to fight. A minor rising of the Wahpeton Sioux in Minnesota in which five settlers were killed quickly escalated into a general uprising in the area, during which the Redwood Agency was attacked and Fort Ridgley and the town of New Ulm besieged. After relief units reached the area on 3 September and defeated the Indians at the Battle of Birch Coulee, a concerted attempt was made to pursue and destroy the remaining Sioux. A month later, the Indians suffered a heavy defeat at the hands of the Union infantry at the Battle of Wood Lake. However, their leaders escaped to the north chased by a volunteer brigade comprising three infantry regiments, an artillery company and the 1st Minnesota Mounted Rangers. Again battle was joined, on this occasion near Bismarck, North Dakota, and again the Indians were roundly defeated. Thereafter Brigadier General Alfred Sully with the 6th Iowa and 2nd Nebraska cavalry regiments was ordered to beat the remaining Sioux into submission, neutralizing them as a fighting force for the rest of the war. On 3 September 1863, a year to the day after the Battle of Birch Coulee, four companies of the 6th Iowa met and were surrounded by 4,000 Sioux braves in the region of Ellendale, North Dakota. A single cavalryman managed to escape the trap to bring word to Sully, who immediately advanced with the rest of his brigade, trapping the unsuspecting Sioux in a ravine. The Indians managed to fight off the cavalry until nightfall when the survivors escaped, leaving some 3,000 warriors dead, wounded, or prisoner. The cavalry lost 22 killed and 50 wounded in the engagement, which subsequently became known as the Battle of Whitestone Hill, and inflicted upon the Sioux their greatest ever defeat at the hands of the U.S. Cavalry.

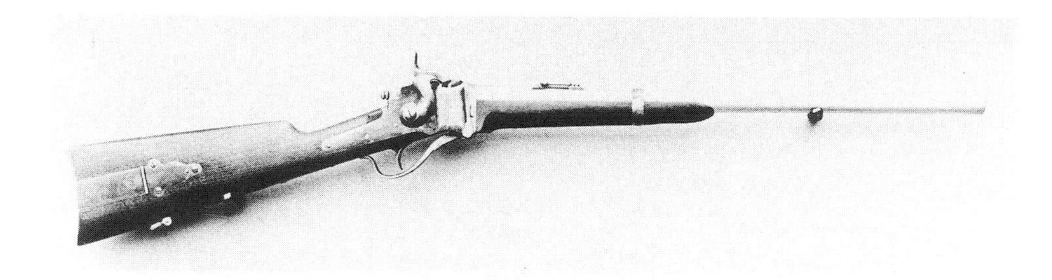

Sharps carbines proved popular with the cavalry on both sides.

In July 1864, Sully – his brigade now reinforced by the 7th Iowa Cavalry, two companies of Dakota cavalry, Brackett's Minnesota Cavalry Battalion, the 2nd Minnesota Cavalry, and some assorted infantry – advanced along the Missouri River intent on destroying once and for all the final vestiges of the Sioux nation. Battle was joined at Killdeer, near the Spring River, on 28 July, and a force of 1,600 braves was routed by a spirited saber charge by Brackett's Minnesotans. Sully continued his relentless advance, reaching the Yellowstone River on 12 August, Fort Berthold on 28 August, and Fort Rice on 8 September.

As the Civil War approached its conclusion, cavalry volunteers from the East, who in the main had enlisted specifically to fight the Confederacy but who were now largely stationed many hundreds of miles from home in the barren wastes of the West, began to agitate to return home. However, not one unit mutinied, while some, notably the 11th Ohio Cavalry which was not disbanded until 12 July 1866, remained in uniform long after the South had surrendered.

THE PENNSYLVANIA RESERVES

Few units in the Federal army epitomized so precisely the effects of the inefficiency and petty mongering of the politicians of 1861 as did the Pennsylvania Reserves. Within days of the attack on Fort Sumter, literally tens of thousands of loyal Unionists offered their services to the colors. The administration, both nationally and at state level, was simply overwhelmed. Anticipating a longer war than that envisaged by the over-optimistic central government, Governor Andrew Curtin of Pennsylvania continued to accept men into service long after Secretary for War Simon Cameron had declared the state's allocation filled. When the jealous and ambitious Cameron refused to accept the new regiments, Curtin "adopted" them by authorizing the creation of a Pennsylvania Reserve Corps, assuming (correctly) that they would soon be inducted into the regular army. Originally designated the 1st to 13th Pennsylvania Reserves, this unique division was eventually accepted into the Union army and renamed the 30th to 42nd Pennsylvania Volunteers. Most soldiers, however, insisted on keeping the old names, causing administrative havoc and confusion wherever they went.

Although it was originally intended that the Reserves would adopt uniforms similar to those of the regular forces, at the time of their induction supplies were exhausted, with the result that the units were forced to remain in "cadet gray" until the end of the war. Quite how many Pennsylvanians were mistaken for the enemy and shot by Union snipers because of this administrative nonsense has never been recorded.

Initially, all 13 regiments were grouped into three brigades and one large division. (The 1st Pennsylvania Cavalry and 1st Pennsylvania Light Artillery were at first also attached to the Reserves Division but were transferred out within a few months.) Originally part of McDowell's I Corps, the division transferred to Porter's V Corps prior to the Peninsula campaign but returned to I Corps in the late summer of 1862, remaining with it throughout the battles of 2nd Manassas (Bull Run), Antietam (Sharpsburg), and Fredericksburg. Having sustained heavy losses, the division was ordered to Washington later that year for rest and recuperation. Almost immediately McCandless's 1st and Fisher's 3rd Brigades requested to be returned to the Army of the Potomac to help in the defense of their own native Pennsylvania which by then had come under serious threat from Lee's advancing Army of Northern Virginia. Assigned to Meade's (later Sykes') V Corps, they were redesignated the 3rd Division under the command of General Samuel Crawford and, as such, fought tenaciously at Gettysburg and in subsequent campaigns. The last action of the Reserves as a unit was at Bethesda Church near Richmond on 1 June 1864.

When the Reserves were mustered out later that month, a large number re-enlisted. Reorganized along with new recruits into the 190th and 191st Pennsylvania Volunteers, collectively designated the Veteran Reserve Brigade, they fought as part of Ayres' Division, V Corps, at Cold Harbor.

Confusingly, brigade organization within the division did not remain a constant. At the Battle of Fredericksburg, McCandless's 1st Brigade incorporated the 1st, 2nd, 6th, and 13th Regiments, Magilton's 2nd Brigade comprised the 3rd, 4th, 7th, and 8th, while Fisher's 3rd accounted for the 5th, 9th,

An attack by the Pennsylvania Bucktails, led by Colonel Thomas Kane, against Stonewall Jackson's Virginians in the woods near Harrisburg, Virginia, on 7 June 1862.

Headdress: As a concession to common sense all Pennsylvania Reserves were issued with standard issue Federal blue kepis.

Tunic: By late 1862 the majority of reserves wore blue tunics although a number retained the original "cadet gray" blouses and the majority still wore gray trousers.

Weapons: Many reserve units, notably the 13th, were recruited from the backwoods and included an unusually large number of excellent shots. Many carried personally acquired sporting rifles in preference to issue muskets. As the war progressed and hand to hand fighting became more common, the once maligned bayonet became more evident.

Company F, 114th Pennsylvania Infantry, pose for a photograph. Note the camouflaged encampment at the rear.

10th, 11th, and 12th. The 1st and 3rd Brigades reformed with the same regiments when they rejoined the Army of the Potomac prior to Gettysburg, whereas the 2nd disbanded. Of its former members, the 3rd and 4th fought with the Army of West Virginia, distinguishing themselves at Cloyd's Mountain (9–10 May 1864), while the 7th and 8th were assigned to the 1st and 3rd Brigades respectively, acquitting themselves with their customary zeal during the Wilderness campaign. Although they were supposed to take part in the same battle, the 9th was found to be so depleted prior to the campaign that it was returned to Washington in May 1864 for premature discharge.

Throughout its history, the Reserves Division was blessed with excellent commanders. Formed initially by George Archibald McCall, a veteran of the Seminole and Mexican wars and an excellent tactician, command passed to John Fulton Reynolds on the division's induction into the Army of the Potomac (although, strangely, it continued to bear McCall's name). General George Meade, later to be victor at Gettysburg, commanded for a short period before his promotion, after which the division passed to Crawford. Although the most famous of its commanders, Meade was arguably the least effective, if only because of his irascible temperament. In the words of General Grant, Meade was "an officer of great merit ... brave and conscientious," yet he "was unfortunately of a temper that would get beyond his control at times ... making it unpleasant at times, even in battle, for those around him to approach him even with information."

To comprehend fully the extent of the Reserves' involvement throughout the war, it is necessary to analyze in more depth the part played by individual regiments.

The 8th Reserves, 37th Pennsylvania Volunteers, was formed in the steel city of Pittsburgh on 28 June 1861. Initially seconded to outpost duties in northern Virginia, it later joined McClellan's forces on the Peninsula. It sustained 230 casualties during the Seven Days' campaign, mainly at Gaines's Mill, and subsequently fought in every major engagement undertaken by the Army of the Potomac throughout the rest of the year. It lost 131 men, almost half its remaining strength, attacking Marye's Heights during the Battle of Fredericksburg. After a short respite in Washington, the regiment rejoined the army, fighting with distinction during the Wilderness campaign and at Spotsylvania, where it lost 17 killed.

The 10th Reserves, 39th Volunteers, were drawn from the intelligentsia of the western part of the state, with "teachers and pupils serving in the ranks together." Company "D" recruited exclusively from the students of Jefferson College, and Company "I" from their rivals at Allegheny College. In the fight for Gaines's Mill, 134 officers and men fell.

The 11th Reserves, 40th Volunteers, suffered the heaviest losses within the division, the eighth highest *pro rata* losses of the entire Union army. Formed in western Pennsylvania, it too fought at Gaines's Mill where it was cut off and forced to surrender. Exchanged in August 1862, it rejoined the Army of the Potomac before it left for the Peninsula. It subsequently sustained such losses during the battles of 2nd Manassas (Bull Run) and South Mountain that it mustered at Antietam (Sharpsburg) fewer than 200 combatants strong. Bolstered by a few recruits and the return of the wounded, the regiment fought at Fredericksburg with 394 officers and men, of whom 211 were killed or wounded.

The 13th Reserves, known as the "Bucktails," were perhaps the most colorful of all the Pennsylvania regiments. Drawn from the farmers and lumbermen of the outer state, many of whom were excellent shots and insisted on providing their own weapons, the outfit was originally known as the Pennsylvania Rifles or the Kane County Rifles after its first colonel; Thomas Kane. Tradition has it that Private James Landregan of "I" Company, spying a deer's hide hanging outside a butcher's shop in Smethport, Pennsylvania where the regiment was then quartered, crossed the street, pulled out a knife, cut off its tail, and tucked it into his hat. Upon his return to headquarters, Colonel Kane, a man well endowed with a sense of humor and with an eye toward creating a tradition, decreed that in future the unit would be known as the "Bucktails." Thereafter every recruit was required to bring with him, as an indication of his marksmanship, the tail of a buck which he had shot. Four companies were seconded with Colonel Kane to the Army of the Shenandoah (against "Stonewall" Jackson), rejoining the regiment prior to the 2nd Battle of Manassas.

The gray uniforms worn by the Reserves differed greatly in style and texture, varying in color from drab or tan-gray to "cadet" light gray. Of the 13,000 pairs of "linen duck" and "undress brown linen" trousers purchased by the state, some would inevitably have found their way to the Reserves. From late 1862, individual members of the 1st to 13th were issued with blue jackets and virtually all with U.S. army dress hats in an attempt to prevent obvious confusion with the enemy, although some remained clad wholly in gray throughout the war.

The gallant charge of Humphrey's Division, including the Pennsylvania Reserves, at Fredericksburg.

GUNNER: HEAVY ARTILLERY

Despite the terrifyingly destructive power of heavy artillery, so aptly named the "God of War" by Napoleon, it was rarely used to its full potential by the Union army. At the outbreak of war, the North had 4,167 pieces of ordnance in its armory, of which a mere 163 were field guns and howitzers. Between 1861 and 1866, 7,892 cannon of all sizes were issued, 1,700 of which were forged in the massive Cold Spring Foundry.

Pre-war artillery techniques were sadly lacking, owing more to the lessons of the Mexican and Seminole wars than to modern innovation. Matters did improve somewhat when Major William Barry, a veteran of both wars and the spirited commanding officer of the 5th U.S. Artillery during its brilliant and successful defense of Fort Pickens at Pensacola, Florida (May 1861), was promoted and appointed Chief of Artillery within the Army of the Potomac. With the full support of McClellan, if not initially of Congress, Barry gathered together every regular artillery unit that could be spared from fortress duties and outlying areas, concentrating them under one command. By the time the Army of the Potomac was ready to take to the field in August 1861, it contained over half of all professional artillery units in the Union army.

Barry was never able fully to convince his masters of the need for independence of thought and action within the artillery. Although, after the Battle of Chancellorsville, the four batteries attached to each division were concentrated into brigades under direct corps command, with a reserve of 100 fieldpieces and 50 heavier guns set up as a reserve to enhance concentration of fire, the peculiar administrative needs of the guns were never fully understood. Staff structure within the artillery simply did not exist, with the result that planning had to be undertaken by experienced officers from the batteries, leaving actual command of the guns to inexperienced juniors or officers considered incompetent for staff duties. Well after the 1st Battle of Manassas (Bull Run), batteries in action were rarely if ever commanded by officers above the rank of major.

Immediately prior to the war, the rifled barrel had been developed and demonstrated but had been almost universally discounted by the ultra-conservative and all-powerful Congressional military lobby. Nor had it been accepted by the field commanders, who felt that the heavy forests where they considered most battles were likely to be fought would render useless the tremendous increase in range and accuracy afforded by rifling. To the traditionalist, artillery was a defensive weapon. Such smoothbores as the 12-pounder Napoleon, introduced from France and built in great numbers in the North, could project an exploding shell 1,200 yards (1,100m) if required, but

A battery of 12-pounder Napoleons dug into a coastal defensive position. As the war progressed, many such sites were abandoned and the guns transferred inland.

Headdress: Heavy artillery N.C.O.s and gunners were issued with standard blue kepis. However, the traditional Jäger horn insignia was replaced by large brass crossed cannon.

Tunic: Conventional trousers and tunics were issued. Red N.C.O.s' chevrons, trouser stripes, officers' frock-coat trim and shoulder tabs and hat cords demonstrated the wearers' membership of the artillery.

Weapons: All ranks were issued with short (26-in) swords. Usually these were abandoned as impractical although in some cases they were replaced with privately acquired cavalry sabers. Most officers carried pistols.

this was never regarded as their prime function. More importantly, and unlike rifled artillery, they could fire grapeshot 400 yards (365m) and canister 200 yards (185m) into the packed ranks of advancing infantry. It was accepted that smoothbore artillery was of little use in the attack. It could not fire into the protected positions of the defenders immediately prior to an attack without inviting heavy counter battery fire nor could it advance with the infantry without severe losses among the crews at the hands of accurate enemy rifle fire.

The standard U.S. heavy artillery at the outbreak of war consisted of:

- 12-, 24-, and 32-pounder howitzers, capable of throwing an explosive projectile high into the air, which would then fall steeply behind breastworks or walls where it might do most damage to an undefended enemy.
- 12-, 18-, and 24-pounder siege guns.
- 8-inch (20cm) and 24-pounder siege howitzers.
- 8-inch, 10-inch (25cm) and 24-pounder siege mortars.
- 32- and 42-pounder coast defense guns.
- 8- and 10-inch Columbiad coast guns.
- 8- and 10-inch coast howitzers.
- 10- and 13-inch (33cm) coast mortars.

The vast majority of heavy guns in use in the mid-19th century were not only smoothbore in manufacture but were constructed of bronze. Attempts had been made to substitute iron for bronze but successes had been rare. Notwithstanding this, and conscious of the large reserves of good ore to be found in the North and West, Washington persevered with the development of cast-iron barrels, commissioning a number of private gunsmiths to carry out independent experiments.

Many of the results were excellent. Captain Thomas Rodman patented the idea of casting an iron smoothbore gun around a water-cooled core, enabling the metal forming the inner part of the barrel to cool and harden first; as the outer layers cooled, it compressed the inner metal, giving it extra strength to withstand the explosive discharge of the shell. Trials carried out by the War Department in the late 1850's, in which a battery of conventional ordnance was tested against a battery of Rodmans, proved conclusively that the new cast-

A battery of heavy mortars, although relatively short-ranged and inaccurate, could deliver a murderous barrage against an enemy defensive emplacement.

iron barrels had a life expectancy more than eight times that of bronze guns. From 1859 onward all larger guns were cast on the Rodman system. Attempts were subsequently made to upgrade existing iron barrels, which until then had exhibited a dangerous propensity for blowing up, by retrofitting iron hoops over the breech ("Brooke" guns), but as is so often the case with stop-gap measures, success was limited.

As the war progressed, the effectiveness of heavy artillery as an offensive force was at last conceded. The traditional smoothbore having neither the range, accuracy, nor versatility for such a role, the necessity for rifling was begrudgingly accepted. Initial attempts by Colonel James and others simply to cut grooves in existing bronze smoothbores merely succeeded in weakening the barrel with inevitable catastrophic consequences for the crews. The most successful rifled gun of the time was the "Armstrong," designed by William Armstrong, an English lawyer turned hydraulic engineer. Wrought-iron hoops were heated and shrunk, one upon another, over the weakest part of the rifled iron barrel to give it additional compressed strength. More fundamentally, and for the first time in the history of heavy ordnance, the weapon was loaded from the breech rather than the muzzle. Although slow and cumbersome by modern standards, the Armstrong was revolutionary for its day and quickly became the model for a series of subsequent Union designs.

The heaviest guns served by the field artillery were the siege mortars: massive stubby weapons transported ponderously about battlefields on simple wooden carriages or, where possible, floated into position on large rafts. When fired from the land, mortars were usually positioned on a flat timber bed to spread the recoil and to offer as smooth a working surface as possible. The direction of fire was roughly estimated by the commander, who aligned a piece of weighted string, held vertically at arm's length and in the direction of the target, with a line painted along the top of the barrel. As the barrel was constantly at a given elevation, usually between 45 and 50 degrees, it was only possible to determine the range by altering the quantity of powder in the cartridge. Perhaps because of, rather than despite, their obvious indiscriminate fall of shot, siege mortars invariably had a devastating effect on civilian morale.

A particularly famous 13-inch siege mortar, nicknamed "Dictator" by its crew, was used by Company "G," the 1st Connecticut Heavy Artillery, between 9 and 31 July 1864, during the Siege of Petersburg. Mounted on a specially constructed railroad flatcar and positioned on a bend in the track to afford it lateral adjustment of fire, the monster hurled 45 200-lb rounds an average distance of 3,600 yards (3,292m) into the heart of the enemy position.

A number of heavy artillery regiments were formed from existing infantry units. The 8th New York Heavy Artillery was formed in December 1862 from the 129th New York Infantry, itself formed the previous August from volunteers from the New York State counties of Niagara, Orleans, and Genesee. Many heavy artillery units on garrison duty converted or, in the case of the 8th New York, reverted to the infantry in May 1864 to assist Grant in his final push against Richmond. In that capacity, despite their obvious lack of training for the role, many served outstandingly. In ten months of action, the 8th New York lost 1,010 in action, of whom 361 were killed, 14 percent of the total complement of 2,575 officers and men. The 1st Maine Heavy Artillery took more casualties than any other unit during the Wilderness campaign losing 600 out of 900 participants in one charge alone.

Unlike their brasher light infantry colleagues, the heavy artillery wore a uniform very similar to that of the basic infantry save for the red of the N.C.O.s' chevrons, trouser stripes, and frock-coat trim, and officers' shoulder straps and hat cords. All ranks were entitled to carry a short, stubby sword based on a French variant of the Roman infantryman's sword, but few bothered. Officers, however, tended to carry a pistol. Large brass crossed cannons were worn in lieu of the infanteers' Jäger horn as a cap badge.

The English 600-pounder Armstrong gun was among the largest to see action during the war.

The interior of Fort Sumter during the initial bombardment.

U.S. SIGNAL CORPS

Despite the obvious necessity for the speedy transmission of orders and intelligence, the Union army did little to exploit the full potential of the telegraph until comparatively late in the war.

At the outbreak of hostilities, the War Department requested the American Telegraph Company, with its established system along the eastern seaboard, and the Western Union Telegraph Company, then expanding westward through the Allegheny Mountains, to provide military communications in the east. Control was vested in Anson Stager, the former general superintendent of Western Union and a close friend of Secretary of War Edwin Stanton. With the willing assistance of Stanton, himself a former director of the Atlantic & Ohio Telegraph Company, but contrary to the wishes of the military who increasingly demanded control of "tactical" or battlefield communications, Stager managed to keep the entire operation civilian. The Federal Military Telegraph System, as it became known, remained answerable to the Secretary of War throughout the conflict, and at no time was control relinquished to the generals.

At its height, the service employed approximately 12,000 telegraphers, transmitted over 3,000 messages a day and maintained 15,000 miles of wire. Attempts were made in March 1864 to force the telegraphers to wear an informal uniform consisting of a dark blue blouse with staff officer's buttons and dark blue trousers with a silver cord down each leg, but there is no evidence that this edict was taken very seriously, particularly in the more remote areas.

Albert James Myer entered the army in 1854 as a medical graduate but soon realized that his talents lay in the embryonic field of communications. Working closely with E.P. Alexander, who was later to transfer his allegiance to the Confederacy, he experimented in depth with Morse code, eventually introducing the "wigwag" signal system. On 27 June 1860, he became the army's first signal officer, a post created by Congress as a reward for his achievements. He at once set about the creation of a formal military Signals Corps. With the advent of war, Myer clashed heavily with Stager whom he regarded as a commercial opportunist. Stager called upon the assistance of his political allies in Washington, as a direct result of which Myer was relieved of his command in November 1863 and was transferred to the West where, it was felt, his views would be less influential. By then, however, the Signal Corps had been firmly established and was proving its worth on every battlefield.

Direct lines were laid from Washington to the principal army headquarters, enabling orders to be transmitted instantaneously. Further lines were laid from army to corps headquarters. Field crews – either civilian or military – accompanied the Corps to ensure that communications were re-established immediately after the headquarters moved into a

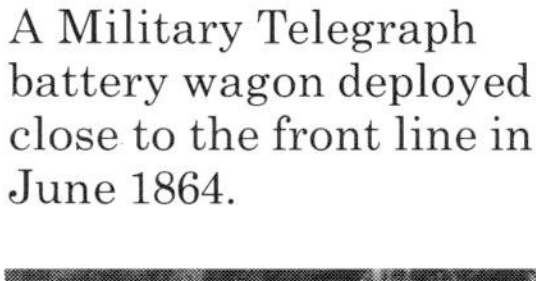

A Military Telegraph battery wagon deployed close to the front line in June 1864.

Headdress: All ranks wore conventional blue kepis. Officers wore a cap badge consisting of an embroidered Signals Corps flag with the letters "US" above the cross within a wreath. Men assigned to the balloon corps often wore the letters "AD" for Aeronautic Department or "BC" for Balloon Corps on their hats.

Tunic: Signallers wore plain dark blue cavalry jackets and trousers and were armed with Colt revolvers. Square crossed flags on 3-in long staffs, one red within a white border, the other white within a red border, were worn on the right upper arm to signify the branch of service.

Crow's nest signals stations were set up behind the front line to ensure the speedy transmission of orders from the rear headquarters.

new position, in this way denying the more maverick of the commanders any excuse for excessive independent action.

Communications to divisions and regiments, at this level totally the prerogative of the military, worked less formally. Telegraphy was used if the terrain permitted and the battle was static, but otherwise traditional visual means were resorted to. Signal officers were attached to each headquarters, to the major artillery batteries, and to observation posts to ensure that details of potential targets reached the guns with minimum delay. Responsibility for the laying and maintenance of lines, often eight miles in length, was delegated to cable detachments commanded by senior N.C.O.s. Reels of field cable were transported on wagons and, because the insulation of the wire was often poor, normally secured to short poles or trees. Mounted telegraphers tapped into the main telegraph routes where possible and attempted thereafter to keep the lines open and secure.

When troop movement was anticipated or the battlelines were fluid, visual signaling – lamps by night and flags by day – was preferred. Although the system had the advantage of simplicity, observation was an obvious drawback. By their very nature, relay posts had to be in the clear line of sight of the recipient and were therefore invariably overlooked by the enemy. Surprisingly, neither semaphore (the use of flags held at different angles to the signaler's body) nor Morse code appear to have been developed within the Signal Corps. Instead, a superficially simple, if chronically slow, system was adopted that demanded the use of only three flag positions in which letters were indicated by reference to the numbers 1, 2, or 3. To indicate the number 1, the signaler would move the flag in a semicircle down to his left. A corresponding movement to the right would indicate 2, and to the front, 3. Letters, and where possible phrases, were represented by a sequence of numbers. Thus "1.1" represented the letter "A," "1.2.2.1" "B," and "3.3" "end of message."

Although this simple expediency was sufficient to protect a message from a casual observer, it could easily be unraveled by anyone with the time and determination. Primitive ciphers, such as that utilizing twin overlapping wheels each with the alphabet inscribed in jumbled form around its edge, were often employed to afford primitive protection. When greater security was required, formal codes were introduced. Given sufficient time and, ideally, the aid of a computer, most codes of today are not considered difficult to break. Fortunately for the Union, however, the Confederacy lacked both the technique and facilities for serious analysis, with the result that the North's communications were never seriously compromised. At night, torches – or less commonly, Coston lights, a series of 20 colored lamps, each with a previously designated meaning – replaced the flags.

Whereas the Confederacy introduced the telegraph system, Union commanders such as Ulysses S. Grant made it their own. Taking his loathing of verbose letters and lengthy reports to its logical conclusion, Grant had whenever possible a telegraph installed in his field office where he would spend much of his time talking by wire to all parts of his command. Each of his brigade headquarters was allotted a line team consisting of two men, a mule and reel of insulated wire; each team was expected to make it its business to maintain contact at all times with army command.

During Sherman's campaign into Georgia, the Military Telegraph was fully stretched maintaining communications. Here the line is extended to Ackworth, Georgia.

Without doubt, the most unusual application of the telegraph was in conjunction with the "lighter than air" balloon. Thaddeus Lowe, a well-known pre-war balloonist, offered his services to the Union, and in 1861, the Balloon Corps was authorized. The following year, seven balloons accompanied McClellan in the Peninsula campaign and soon proved their worth both as intelligence gatherers and as spotters for the guns. Each balloon required a squad of men to maintain its generator (which used a dangerous combination of sulfuric acid and iron filings to generate the hydrogen gas), fill the canopy and attend to the tethering ropes. Initially, these men were drawn from the ranks of the Topographical Engineers on the dubious premise that map-making seemed an obvious application, but soon administration passed first to the Military Telegraph Corps and then to the Quartermaster's Department before inevitably reverting to the Signal Corps. Shortsightedly, the Corps complained to the War Department that it had neither the men nor the finances to run the balloons, as a result of which the Balloon Corps was disbanded. The Confederacy breathed a sigh of relief and the Union lost one of its finest assets.

There was very little to differentiate a signaler from a line soldier except for the former's $\frac{3}{4}$-inch (12cm) square crossed signals flags – one red within a white border, the other white within a red border – on 3-inch (7.5cm) long staffs that were worn on the upper sleeve. In the field, the men wore standard cavalry jackets and trousers and were armed with Colt revolvers for personal protection. Officers wore a cap badge consisting of embroidered Signals Corps flags surmounted by the letters "US" within a wreath. Troops attached to the balloons would occasionally provide added panache by wearing the letters "AD" denoting ("Aeronautic Department") or "BC" for ("Balloon Corps") on their hats.

THE IRON BRIGADE OF THE WEST

Few units served the Union cause as bravely or tenaciously as the Iron Brigade of the West. Originally comprising the 19th Indiana and 2nd, 6th, and 7th Wisconsin regiments and later joined by the 24th Michigan, the brigade recruited exclusively from the Midwest. Over half of its membership consisted of native Americans, 40 percent were Scandinavians or Irish, the residue being of German or English extraction.

The brigade saw action at the 1st and 2nd Battles of Manassas (Bull Run), sustaining one-third casualties, and throughout the Maryland campaign, where during three weeks of bitter fighting it lost 58 percent of its remaining strength. At Antietam (Sharpsburg), a war correspondent, sickened by the carnage yet mindful of the considerable part played by these Midwestern troops in the North's first victory, christened the brigade the "Iron Brigade," ignorant of the fact that that title had earlier been bestowed on Hatch's New Yorkers; nevertheless, the name stuck. After fighting at Fredericksburg and Chancellorsville, the Iron Brigade threw itself unreservedly into the Gettysburg campaign, losing two-thirds of the 1,800 who fought on Seminary Ridge. The soul if not the body of the Iron Brigade of the West died at Gettysburg, and although it continued to function as an independent unit, it was destined not to play any further major part in the war.

Throughout its existence, the brigade was blessed with several brilliant commanding officers. Responsibility for its initial formation was delegated to Rufus King, a retired railroad engineer, newspaper editor, and one time Attorney-General for New York State. In 1861, King had been appointed Minister to the Vatican but, fortunately for the Union, had delayed his voyage, sensing that his services would soon be required closer to home. According to the traditions of the day, King was given command of his brigade leading it successfully until his promotion to major general in March 1862. Brigadier John Gibbon, who succeeded King, was without doubt one of the finest tacticians of the war. A veteran of the Seminole War and a former West Point artillery instructor, Gibbon denied his family ties at the outbreak of hostilities, turned his back on his three brothers then fighting for the Confederacy, and threw in his lot with the North. Initially gazetted commanding major of Battery "B," 4th U.S. Artillery in support of King's brigade, Gibbon was soon appointed Chief of Artillery, Army of the Potomac. Promoted to brigadier general in May 1862, he assumed command of the brigade, a post which he retained until his elevation to major general the following November. Although subsequently badly wounded, Gibbon refused to retire from active service, returning to the fray with renewed vigor after a period of

The Iron Brigade of the West sustained one-third casualties during hand-to-hand fighting at Bull Run.

Headdress: By 1862 a standard Federal blue uniform had been issued to the brigade. This included a large black "Hardee" hat which earned the brigade its alternative nickname, "The Black Hat Brigade."

Hat badge: As supplies ran out, the original ornate regimental hat badges were replaced by more conventional Federal issue. Company B, the 6th Wisconsins depicted here, sustained horrific losses at Spotsylvania.

Footwear: Issue white gaiters were soon abandoned as impractical. Cheap and uncomfortable issue boots were usually replaced by civilian footwear purchased privately or looted from Confederate prisoners.

sick leave. Appointed one of the surrender commissioners at Appomattox and breveted for his actions at Antietam, Fredericksburg, Spotsylvania, and Petersburg, Gibbon returned to the postwar regular artillery in the rank of colonel, seeing extensive service on the frontier. One of his final actions as an officer was to lead the relief column to the Little Big Horn in 1876 to bury the mutilated remains of his friend, Colonel (formerly General) George Custer.

Gibbon having been promoted, command passed to Solomon Meredith, a pre-war public office holder and a blatant political appointee. Meredith had, however, successfully led the 19th Indiana since its inception, had been wounded while leading his troops from the front at Groveton, and turned out to be an excellent choice. Described by a colleague as "six feet six inches in height, of commanding presence, and a ready speaker," he was seriously injured on the second day of Gettysburg and never fully recovered from his injuries nor from the fact that two of his three sons serving with the Union were killed. Mustered out in May 1865, Meredith accepted the post of Surveyor-General of Montana before retiring to a farming life.

Each of the commanders stamped his own authority on the individualistic and somewhat eccentric dress of the brigade. Although officers were issued with standard U.S. army uniforms, there was insufficient material to clothe all the volunteers in blue on the outbreak of war. The 2nd Wisconsin were therefore equipped with plain, single-breasted gray frock coats, gray trousers with a black cord down each leg, a gray kepi trimmed with black and a gray overcoat trimmed with black piping and pockets. The 6th Wisconsin originally mustered in a motley assortment of civilian dress comprising a colorful mixture of cloth and headwear totally inapproriate to war. Before leaving their home

Antietam Bridge, where the Iron Brigade lost 72 out of 200 fighting men during one fierce battle.

state, they were issued with gray single-breasted jackets with black shoulder straps, cuffs, and collars, plain gray forage caps, gray trousers with a black strip down each leg, and a gray overcoat. The material was, however, of such poor quality that within a month the majority of uniforms were in shreds, compelling the 6th to enter Washington once again civilianized save for a "uniform" consisting of "gray hats trimmed with green."

Inevitably, the volunteer gray uniforms of both regiments were often mistaken for the more regulated apparel of the Confederate infantry, with dire results: during the 1st Battle of Manassas (Bull Run), the 2nd Wisconsins were forced to withdraw in disorder, having declined until too late to fire on the advancing enemy under the misconception that they were friendly reinforcements. After the battle, the entire brigade was quickly issued dark blue frock coats and sky-blue trousers. Gibbon, on taking command, had the brigade issued with distinctive black "Hardee" hats and white gaiters. The ravages of battle soon took their toll, and by 1863, over half of the brigade had abandoned the frock coat in favor of the more durable fatigue coat. The impractical gaiters were soon discarded as were the ornate hat badges, but the "Hardee" hat itself remained as a jealously guarded and distinctive feature, earning the unit the nickname of the "Black Hat Brigade." Inexplicably, some officers preferred the kepi while the 24 Michigan, which was posted in immediately before Antietam, remained loyal to the conventional uniform of fatigue cap and blouse.

The Iron Brigade at Gettysburg. Note the distinctive headgear of the leading officer.

Few brigades fought in as many campaigns or sustained the losses of the Iron Brigade of the West. Organized in Indianapolis on 29 July 1861 following the briefest of training, the 19th Indiana joined the main army in Washington on 5 August. It lost 259 out of a strength of 423 at 2nd Manassas, 53 at South Mountain, and 72 out of 200 combatants at Antietam: 210 officers and men from a total of 288 engaged fell at Gettysburg, and a further 226 in the fighting from the Wilderness to Petersburg. (For more information on the 19th Indiana, see p. 64.) The Wisconsin regiments fared no better, the 2nd suffering the highest percentage of losses in the Union army: 19.7 percent killed. Of a total enrollment of 1,203, the regiment lost 753 killed and wounded, 132 missing or captured (of whom 17 died in prison), and 60 nonbattle casualties from disease and injury. After Spotsylvania, losses were so great that the regiment, now reduced to fewer than 100 active men, was ordered home and mustered out, the survivors being transferred to Companies "A" and "B" of the 6th Wisconsins after a period of initial recuperation serving, in the opinion of the men rather wastefully, as a headquarters provost guard with the 4th Division. The Iron Brigade of the West should not be confused with John Porter Hatch's "Iron Brigade," comprising the 2nd U.S. Sharpshooters and the 22nd, 24th, 30th, and 84th New York Volunteers, with whom they served as part of King's division at the 2nd Battle of Manassas. Hatch's "Iron Brigade" was broken up in May 1863 when the 22nd, 24th, and 30th New York were mustered out at the expiration of their two years' service.

SUPPORT TROOPS

Within four years of the outbreak of war, the US army grew from a parochial force of 16,000 officers and men to a monolithic 2 million. Standards of support and administration which had sufficed for a professional army in peacetime were simply inadequate for the logistical needs of a part-volunteer, part-conscript force in time of war. Men who would never have passed the stringent medical examination for the regulars were accepted *en masse*, straining to breaking point the limited medical facilities available. Those who would once have been forced through age or injury to retire were now posted to the Veteran Reserve Corps to guard strategically important posts.

Although the troops became hardened and professional by their experiences in combat, and some became brutalized, it was important for the maintenance of their morale to ensure that they retained, whenever possible, memories of home and the cause for which they were fighting. Newspapers did much to bring the full extent of the war to the civilian population. Circulation among the great Northern dailies increased considerably as each tried to outstrip its rivals in the production of timely and accurate war news. Corps of "special" correspondents followed the armies and the navy, providing volumes of information and vivid feature items which were read as avidly by the troops – the vast majority of whom, in the best traditions of fighting men, had little idea of where they were, where they were going or why – as by those back home. Graphic battlefield maps, usually better than those available to the army, were compiled by highly skilled cartographers and reproduced faithfully on the front pages of such papers as the *New York Herald*. Overt censorship appears not to have existed, but then neither was there much to censor, although whether this was due to journalistic patriotism or the readerships' jingoistic refusal to accept detailed criticism of such notables as President Lincoln remains a moot point.

The spiritual welfare of troops facing death and mutilation on a regular basis was not forgotten. In all, 2,500 chaplains were employed by the Union army, of whom 11 were killed in action. On 22 July 1864, one of their number, the Rev. Milton Haney attached to the 55th Illinois Infantry, was awarded the Congressional Medal of Honor, the highest award for valor in the face of the enemy, for his part in the Battle for Atlanta. In 1862, for the first time in United States military history, Jewish rabbis were allowed into the chaplains' ranks.

Under the terms of an order promulgated on 25 November 1861, chaplains were to wear plain black frock coats with a standing collar and a single row of nine black buttons, plain black pantaloons and a plain unadorned black hat or forage cap, the last item replaced by a plain *chapeau-bras* for

As the war progressed, limited Federal supplies were often supplemented by booty captured from the Confederacy.

Headdress: Plain unadorned black hats, decorated after August 1864 with a staff officer's cap badge, were replaced by a *chapeau-bras* on ceremonial occasions.

Frock coat: Chaplains were expected to wear plain black frock coats with standing collars and a single row of nine black buttons. However, as they were expected to purchase their own clothing, many elected to appear in far more eccentric attire.

Weapons: Although not obligatory, a number of chaplains carried straight swords. Many chaplains saw active service; eleven were killed in action and one awarded the Congressional Medal of Honor.

ceremonial purposes. On 25 August 1864, this rather plain uniform was enhanced by the addition of "herring-bone" or black braid around the buttons and button holes and a staff officers' cap badge. In reality, however, as chaplains had to equip themselves and were usually considered as an unwanted impediment by all but the most devout commanders, they were rarely taken to task for wearing non-regulation uniforms, and they soon gained the unenviable reputation of being the most eccentric dressers in the army. Since chaplains received the pay of a cavalry captain, many wore captain's shoulder straps which, together with the straight sword favored by some, made them look faintly ridiculous. In the words of the lieutenant colonel commanding the 127th Pennsylvania Volunteer Infantry on seeing his new chaplain Captain Gregg approaching the camp for the first time, resplendent in "a new uniform with prominent shoulder straps, a regulation hat with a gold circulet, and a gold cord, sashed, belted and spurred, and with a sword dangling at his side: 'What damn fool is that?' "

The regular supply of fresh food and water was of cardinal importance if the troops, particularly the less-acclimatized urban dwellers, were not to succumb to disease which, despite precautions, accounted for a staggering 224,586 Union army deaths throughout the war. Military store-keepers, or "suttlers", were appointed to each camp to regulate the supply of provisions. Inevitably, with the huge possibilities for fraud and corruption, particularly in the early stages of the war, standards varied greatly. Store-keepers were authorized "a citizen's frock coat of blue cloth, with buttons of the department to which they are attached; round black hat; pantaloons and vest, plain, white or dark blue; cravat or stock, black." There is evidence, however, that many, particularly those serving in outlying areas, reverted to civilian apparel.

Pay, although never high, was critical to morale. Nevertheless, although soldiers in the field were meant to be paid every two months, most considered themselves lucky if they received payment at four-month intervals, while delays of six and even eight months were not unusual. Union privates received $13.00 per month until June 1864 when this paltry sum was increased to $16.00. N.C.O.s received, on average, an additional $3.00 per rank scale, although specialists, notably engineers received considerably more. Second lieutenants in the infantry or artillery received the far more rewarding salary of $105.50 per month increasing to $115.50 for captains, $169.00 for majors, $181.00 for lieutenant colonels and $212.00 for colonels. General officers of one-, two- and three-star status received $315.00, $457.00 and $758.00 respectively, while staff officers received an average enhancement of $15.00 per month. Little if any benefit seems to have been set aside for retirement or invalidity.

Nearly everything needed by the army, save for weapons and food, was supplied by the Quartermaster Bureau. Uniforms, greatcoats, shoes, haversacks, canteens, mess kit, and blankets were all issued as were barracks, horses, pack mules, and forage. Fresh water for drinking and wood for fuel were brought forward by wagon or, where possible, by ship to insure that the troops at the front remained at all times functional. Invading Northern armies had to maintain long supply lines of wagon trains, railroads, and port facilities. With the exception of those few instances in which the troops lived off the countryside, an invading Union army required one wagon for every 40 men, and one horse, including cavalry remounts, for every two or three men. A campaigning army of 100,000 therefore required no fewer than 2,500 supply wagons, at least 35,000 animals, and over 600 tons of supplies per day.

Control of the Quartermaster Corps was vested in Montgomery C. Meigs, a brilliant and resourceful engineer who assumed the appointment of Quatermaster General in the rank of brigadier on 15 May 1861. Throughout the war, Meigs oversaw the spending of $1.5 billion, virtually half of the North's entire budget. He forced the field armies to abandon their large and heavy Sibley and Adams tents in favor of the far more practical portable shelters known affectionately as "dog" or "pup" tents, introduced standard graduated measurements for uniforms, and pioneered the introduction of the Blake-McKay leather-sewing machine which did much to improve the standards of footwear, particularly among the enlisted ranks of the infantry.

Food and forage were supplied by the Commissary Department. Initial allocations were made by the Commissary-General to the commissaries of armies, which were responsible for the distribution downward to the individual corps, divisions, bri-

The Quartermaster's Office, Fort Fisher.

gades, and regiments. Rations varied but usually consisted of ham, bacon, beef (salted or on the hoof), beans, flour, salt, sugar, coffee, hardtack, and occasionally, especially in the later stages of the war, bread freshly baked by mobile bakeries. Salt was issued in large quantities to prevent fresh meat from putrifying in the heat. Except when it could be pillaged from enemy farmsteads or bought locally, fresh fruit seemed to be wholly lacking, a factor which almost certainly helped the spread of disease.

Artillery, small arms, and all types of ammunition were supplied by the U.S. Ordnance Board. An ordnance officer or sergeant was posted to each regiment and tasked with the completion of weekly returns showing the state of arms, and ready-use and stored ammunition. Most ordnance N.C.O.s were highly experienced and, in many instances, were veterans. Usually they wore full infantry dress uniform with red chevrons surmounted, in the case of fully trained ordnance sergeants, by a distinctive red star.

A Federal supply column is drawn up awaiting orders to advance. The sheer logistics of moving so vast a force were horrendous.

THE PRISONER OF WAR

In four years of bloody and protracted fighting, an estimated 60,250 prisoners of war died in captivity, the vast majority during the final few months of hostilities. During the early stages of the war, prisoners were not a problem. Obsolete forts, derelict factories, converted warehouses, and even county jails were used as makeshift stockades to hold the prisoners while highly informal local arrangements were made between the respective field commanders for their exchange and ultimate release.

As the war progressed and prisoners became more of a burden, the South, already suffering the first privations of the blockade, pressed the Union for a more formal exchange cartel. Initially, Lincoln refused to agree, arguing that to do so would be to recognize the legitimacy of the Confederate government. However, massive Federal losses in the winter battles of 1861–62 heightened Northern public opinion in favor of regularized exchanges, forcing the President to enter into a formal agreement with the enemy army, although technically not with its government. Under the terms of the cartel, which was promulgated on 22 July 1862, each rank was awarded a weighting. An N.C.O. was equivalent to two privates, a lieutenant to four, a captain to six, a major to eight, a lieutenant colonel to ten, a colonel to 15, a brigadier to 20 and a general to 40. Surprisingly, the worth of a commanding general was deemed to be only 60 times that of his newest recruit. Prisoners were exchanged on a one-for-one basis and were subsequently allowed to return to the ranks. Any surplus of prisoners held by either side were released as parolees and, as such, were not allowed to return to active service until formally exchanged. This somewhat unusual system worked so smoothly over the next few months that by the spring of 1863 it was reported that the prisons were empty of all except those too sick or wounded to travel.

The cartel was suddenly suspended in May 1863 when the Confederate Congress endorsed a policy of re-enslavement or execution of black soldiers captured in Union uniform. Although informal exchanges continued thereafter, the whole policy was abandoned by Washington later that year when it was discovered that a significant number of the 30,000 parolees "freed" by Grant after his capture of Vicksburg in July had been returned to duty without formal exchange, in blatant breach of their parole conditions.

Subsequent attempts to renew the cartel foundered when the Confederacy refused either to admit its culpability over the Vicksburg incident or to treat freed slaves within the Union army as bona

Federal prisoners captured during the Second Battle of Bull Run. Virtually no resources existed for their welfare.

Prisoners were held at the mercy and whim of their captors. Many had the better items of their clothing, together with their personal possessions, looted at the time of capture, and were forced to make and mend and even steal from the dead to survive. Medical facilities were largely non-existent. Unknown thousands died needlessly of starvation, disease and neglect on both sides. In 1866 Henry Wirz, the commandant of the Confederate prison at Andersonville, was tried and became the first United States citizen to be executed for war crimes.

fide prisoners of war. Indeed, there is a strong suggestion that attitudes hardened considerably throughout the South, even among the more liberal non-slave-owning urban majority, when it was realized that the Union was willing to use freed slaves against it. As a belated gesture, the Confederate Bureau of War did offer to treat properly black soldiers lawfully freed at the time of their enlistment (but not runaways), but by this stage Northern attitudes were such that no compromise was accepted.

Actual treatment of black prisoners at the hands of the Confederacy varied. Indeed, because the South refused to recognize the status of Negro captives, precise records were not kept and it is therefore virtually impossible even to gain an approximation of how many there were. Some Confederate commanders treated all prisoners alike, while others condoned – and in a few instances, actively organized – massacres. Hundreds of blacks were murdered at Poison Spring, the Crater, and elsewhere. In the two days of carnage which followed the Confederate recapture of Plymouth, North Carolina in April 1864, every black person found in a Union uniform or suspected of supporting the North was slaughtered. Black prisoners spared immediate execution were often returned to their previous masters or occasionally sold to a new one. While awaiting transportation, many were put to hard labor repairing and constructing Confederate defenses.

The worst instances of racial brutality took place on 12 April 1864 after Brigadier General James Chalmers with 1,500 troops recaptured Fort Pillow in western Tennessee from a mixed Union force under the command of Major Lionel Booth. The exact circumstances of the final assault on the fort which immediately preceded the massacre are hotly disputed, but there is some suggestion that Union troops either deliberately or inadvertently fired on a flag of truce. What is certain is that in the ensuing fighting, 231 Union troops were killed and 100 seriously injured for the loss of 14 Confederates killed and 86 wounded. Southern reports suggest that the Union sustained the majority of its losses when its troops attempted a last desperate retreat to the safety of a gunboat patrolling the Mississippi. Federal reports, however, claim that the Union troops, recognizing the impossibility of their position, surrendered as soon as the perimeter defenses of the fort had been breached, and that thereafter the Confederates entered into an orgy of killing, murdering black prisoners, burying others alive, and torching the hospital tents containing their wounded. Whatever the truth, from the moment the story of Fort Pillow became common knowledge until the end of the war, black troops fought the Southern enemy with a previously unknown hatred and ferocity.

President Lincoln was placed on the horns of a dilemma by such Confederate activities. At first, he threatened an eye-for-an-eye retaliation including the execution of a number of Southern troops drawn at random in response to the Fort Pillow massacre. Then he prevaricated and, finally, he did nothing, arguing that such executions would inevitably involve innocent parties and would only serve to strengthen Southern resolve and probably lead to greater and worse retaliation. Despite this, certain Union field commanders in South Carolina and Virginia did carry out their own form of reta-

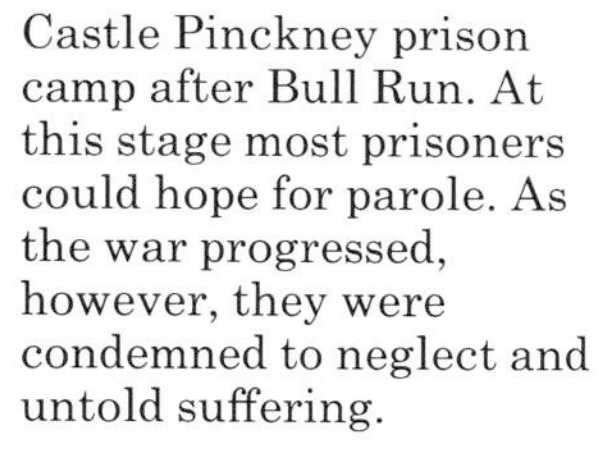

Castle Pinckney prison camp after Bull Run. At this stage most prisoners could hope for parole. As the war progressed, however, they were condemned to neglect and untold suffering.

New York Zouave prisoners at Castle Pinckney prison camp. The sign above the door would indicate that, despite everything, they were able to keep a sense of humour.

liation. When black prisoners were put to work repairing Southern defenses under fire, an equal number of Confederate prisoners were put to work on Union defenses under the same conditions until the practice ceased.

Whereas threats of retaliation did little to help recaptured runaways, there is evidence to suggest that it did much to alter the attitude of the Confederacy toward black freedmen. During the final months of the war, as a prelude to the introduction of conscription among its own slave force, the Confederacy changed its policy toward black prisoners, granting them all prisoner of war status (although not always equal treatment). However, by then it was too late to undo the damage caused by four years of overt racism.

Conditions in Confederate prison camps deteriorated considerably as the North's grip on the South tightened and food became even more scarce. Although there is evidence that prisoners often ate as well as their equally hungry guards, the former inhabitants of the Industrial North seemed less robust than their Southern rural enemies and many died of starvation.

The camp at Andersonville in southwest Georgia came to epitomize the very worst of prison life. Hastily built in February 1864 to accommodate captives previously held on Belle Isle in the James River near Richmond, Andersonville soon became overcrowded with prisoners from Sherman's army as well as from the eastern theater. Initially it was intended that the compound would cover 16 acres and contain sufficient hutted accommodation for 10,000 prisoners. When it was captured in April 1865, it encompassed 26 acres, much of it swamp, and held over 33,000 men. No huts were ever built. Instead, the inmates tried to protect themselves from the heat of the Georgia sun by manufacturing shelters from branches taken from the trees used to construct the outer perimeter fence. The water supply consisted of a single stream which ran sluggishly through the center of the camp, sanitation was provided by a single open sewer, and medical supplies were non-existent. No one knows exactly how many died of starvation, disease, and neglect in Andersonville, although 12,912 bodies lie in the adjoining national cemetery. After the war, the camp commandant, a Swiss immigrant named Henry Wirz, was tried and executed for war crimes.

Not all Confederate prisons were inhumane. Food, sanitation, and accommodation at Camp Ford, built near Tyler, Texas in 1863, were so good that it was not considered necessary to construct a separate hospital block.

Despite the far better living conditions in the North, Federal stockades were often little better than Andersonville. Elmira Prison in New York was designed to hold 5,000 prisoners but in reality held twice that number. Half enjoyed hutted accommodation but the rest were forced to live in tents with not even one blanket each, even during the rigors of mid-winter. Five percent of the inmates per month died of cold and starvation.

Although it is popular to regard Confederate prisons as far worse than those in the North, it should be remembered that the vast majority of postwar historians on whom we must rely for a proper analysis were strongly pro-Union. It is perhaps enough to note that 13 percent of Southern prisoners died in Northern camps compared with only 8 percent of Northerners in Confederate camps.

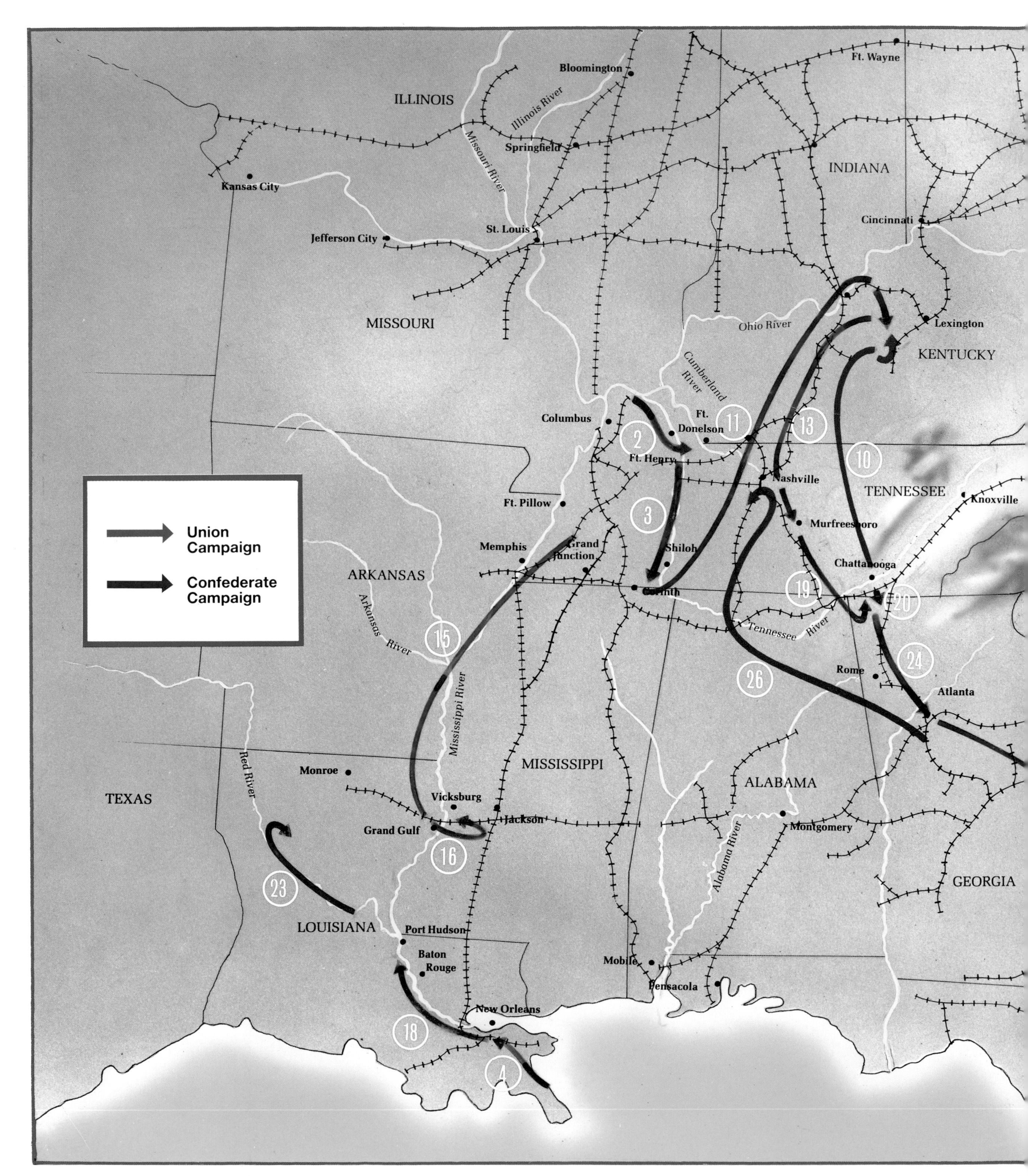
ILLINOIS
Bloomington
Illinois River
Missouri River
Springfield
Ft. Wayne
INDIANA
Kansas City
Cincinnati
Jefferson City
St. Louis
MISSOURI
Ohio River
Lexington
KENTUCKY
Cumberland River
Columbus
Ft. Donelson
Ft. Henry
Nashville
TENNESSEE
Knoxville
Ft. Pillow
Union Campaign
Confederate Campaign
Memphis
Grand Junction
Shiloh
Murfreesboro
ARKANSAS
Arkansas River
Corinth
Chattanooga
Tennessee River
Rome
Atlanta
Mississippi River
TEXAS
Red River
Monroe
MISSISSIPPI
ALABAMA
Vicksburg
Jackson
Grand Gulf
Montgomery
Alabama River
GEORGIA
LOUISIANA
Port Hudson
Baton Rouge
Mobile
Pensacola
New Orleans
2
3
4
10
11
13
15
16
18
19
20
23
24
26

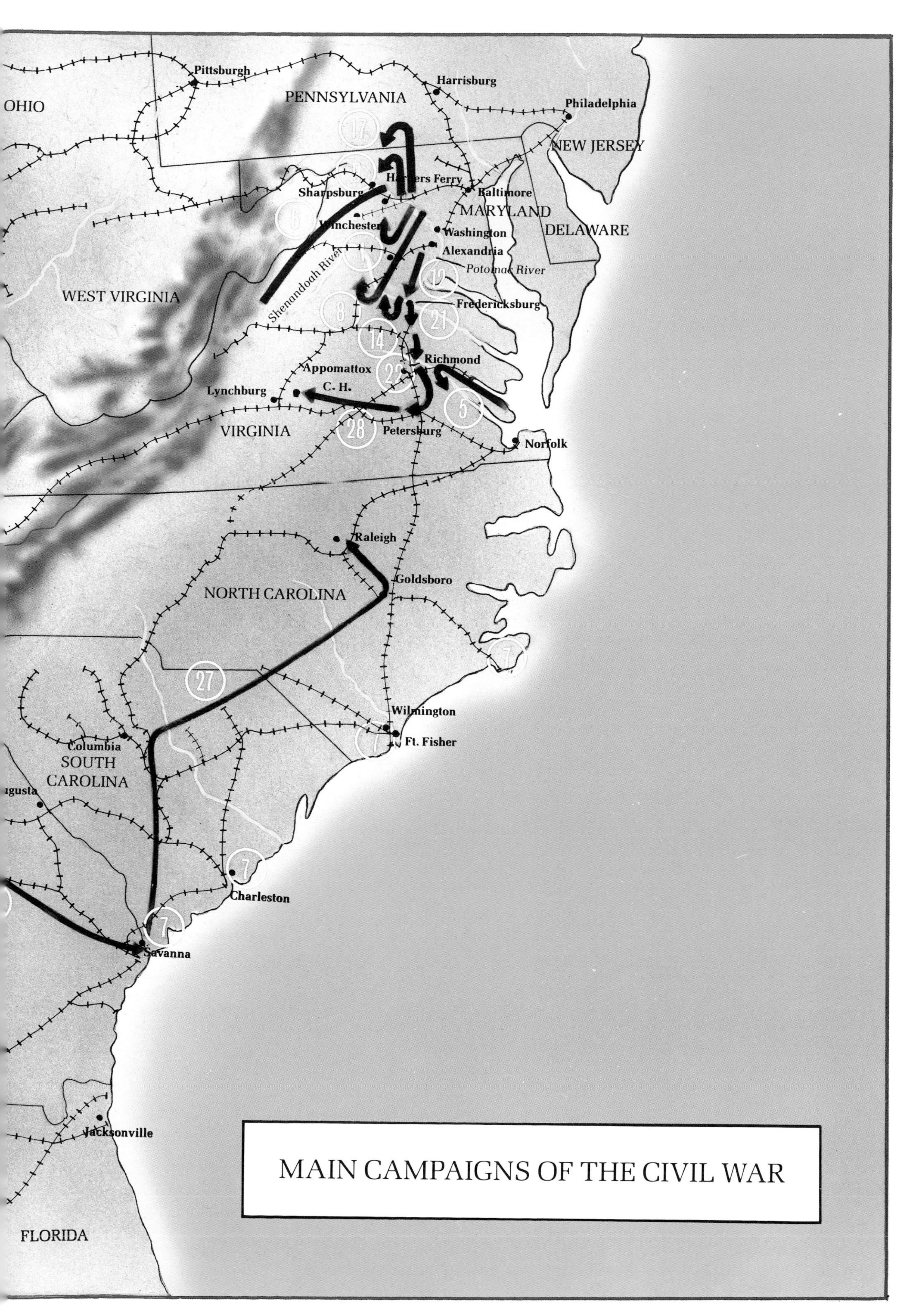

MAIN CAMPAIGNS OF THE CIVIL WAR

1. First Bull Run: McDowell and the Union suffer a rude awakening (July 1861)
2. Grant captures Forts Henry and Donelson (February 1862)
3. Grant defeats the Confederates at Shiloh (April 1862)
4. Farragut's bombardment of New Orleans (April 1862)
5. The Peninsular Campaign (1862)
6. Jackson's Shenandoah Valley Campaign (1862)
7. U.S. Navy blockades Southern Ports (1862)
8. Second Bull Run, and a second victory for the South (1862)
9. Antietam: Lee's invasion of the North ends at Sharpsburg (1862)
10. Bragg's Invasion of Kentucky (1862)
11. Buell marches northeast to meet Bragg at Perryville (1862)
12. Burnside leads the Army of the Potomac to Fredericksburg (1862)
13. Murfreesboro (Stones River) Campaign (1862–63)
14. Chancellorsville (1863): Stonewall Jackson's last charge
15. Grant and Sherman's Vicksburg Campaign (1862–63)
16. The Siege of Vicksburg (July 1863)
17. The Gettysburg Campaign: Lee launches a second invasion (1863)
18. Banks' siege of Port Hudson (July 1863)
19. Rosecrans leads the Union Army to defeat at Chickamauga (September 1863)
20. Reinforced by Grant, the Union Army turns defeat to victory at Chattanooga (October 1863)
21. The Wilderness Campaign begins (Spring 1864)
22. Grant moves south to Spotsylvania (1864)
23. Banks' Red River Campaign (April 1864)
24. The Atlanta Campaign (Summer 1864) ends in Sherman's defeat of Hood and the destruction of Atlanta
25. Promising to "make Georgia howl", Sherman begins his famed "March to the Sea" (November 1864)
26. The Franklin-Nashville Campaign – the South's last hope (1864)
27. The Carolinas Campaign: turning north, Sherman chases Johnston to inevitable defeat (1865)
28. Grant pursues Lee to surrender at Appomattox Court House (April 1865)

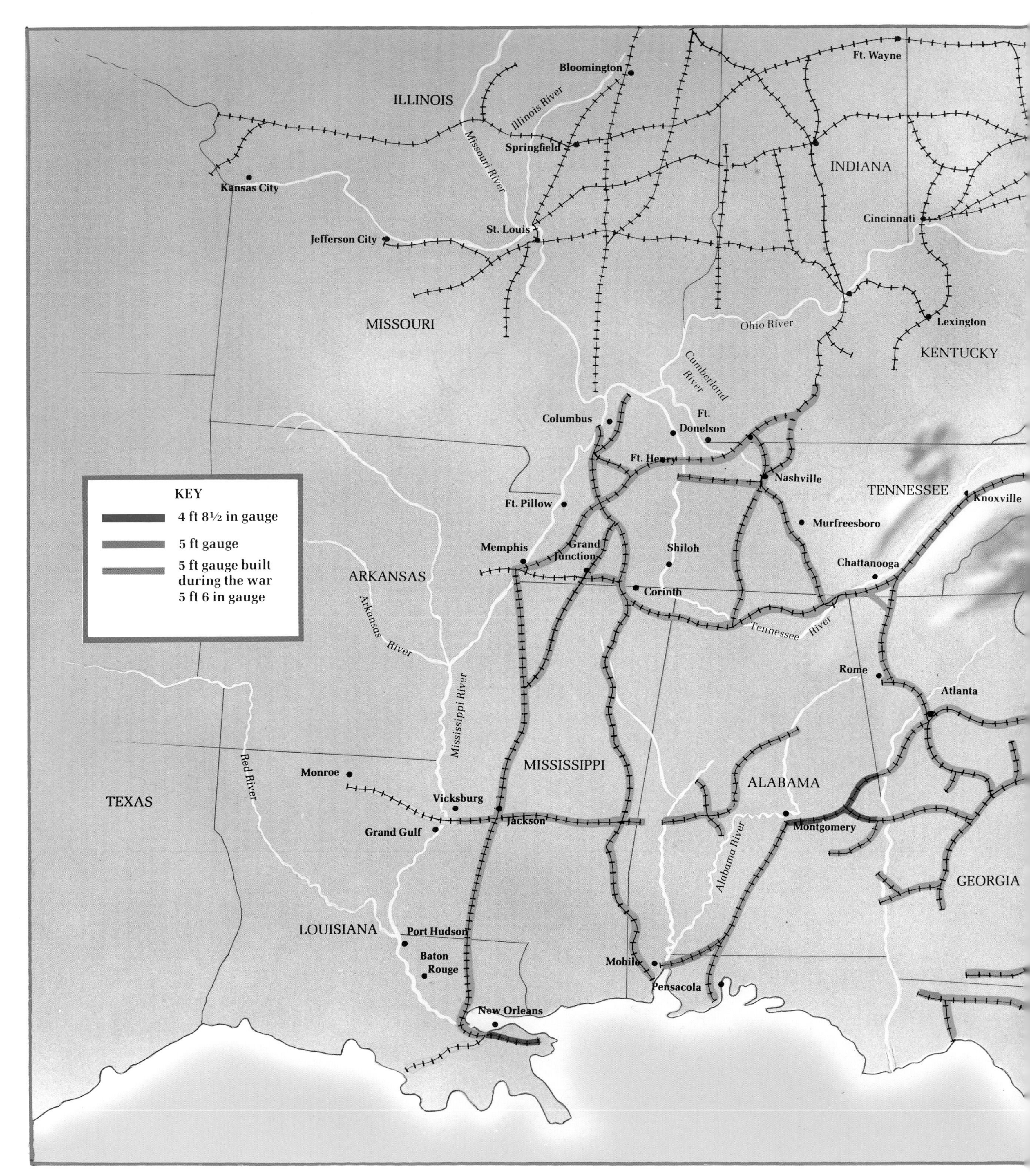
KEY
4 ft 8½ in gauge
5 ft gauge
5 ft gauge built during the war
5 ft 6 in gauge
ILLINOIS
Bloomington
Illinois River
Missouri River
Springfield
Kansas City
Jefferson City
St. Louis
MISSOURI
Ft. Wayne
INDIANA
Cincinnati
Ohio River
Lexington
KENTUCKY
Cumberland River
Columbus
Ft. Donelson
Ft. Henry
Nashville
TENNESSEE
Knoxville
Ft. Pillow
Murfreesboro
Memphis
Grand Junction
Shiloh
Chattanooga
Corinth
ARKANSAS
Arkansas River
Tennessee River
Rome
Atlanta
Mississippi River
TEXAS
Red River
Monroe
Vicksburg
MISSISSIPPI
ALABAMA
Jackson
Grand Gulf
Montgomery
Alabama River
GEORGIA
LOUISIANA
Port Hudson
Baton Rouge
Mobile
Pensacola
New Orleans

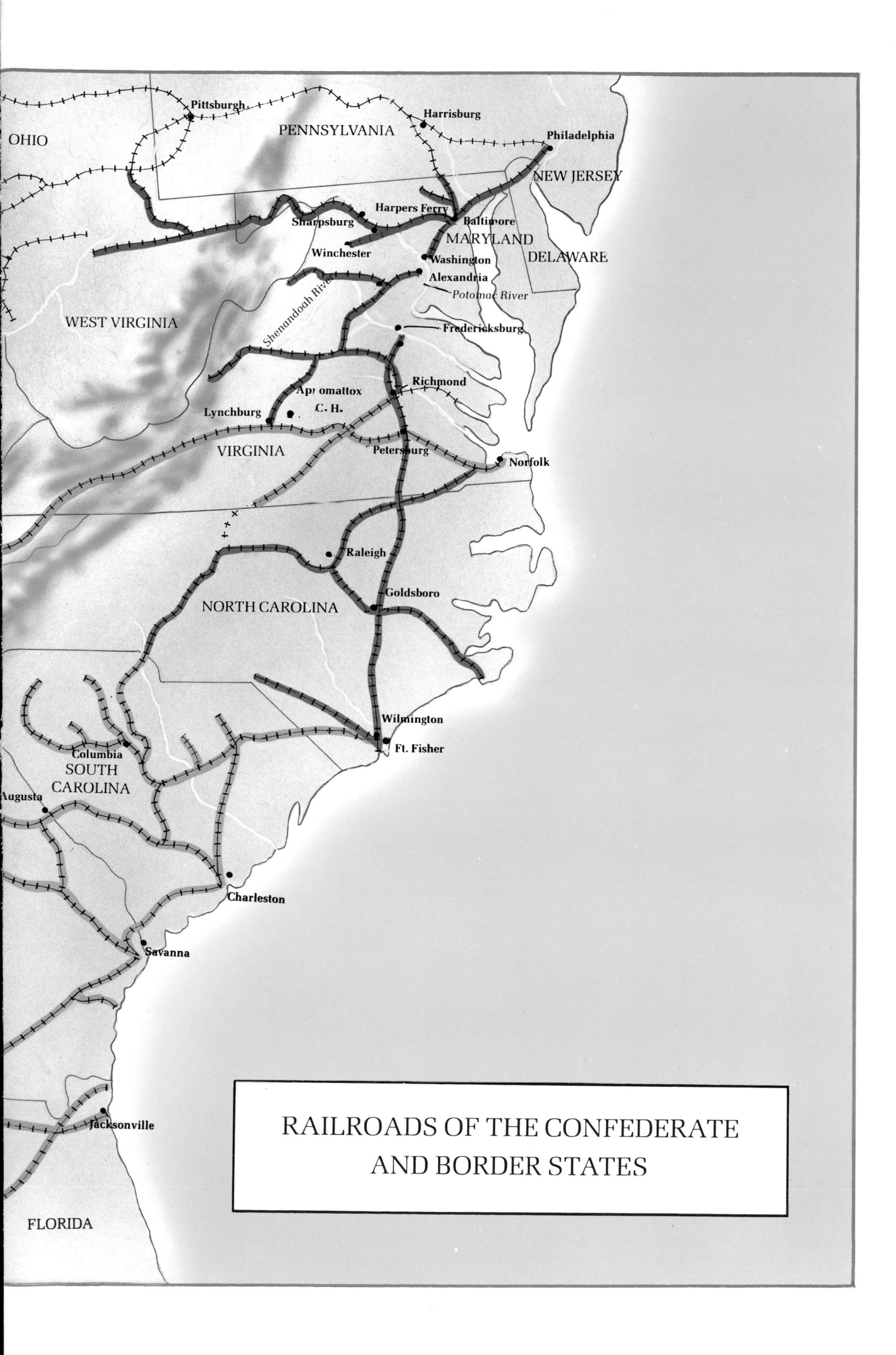

RAILROADS OF THE CONFEDERATE AND BORDER STATES

The First Battle of Bull Run (Manassas) was a bloody introduction to the realities of modern war. McDowell advanced his tired and raw Federal troops against the waiting Confederates with no clear indication of the enemy dispositions. More fundamentally he was unaware that Johnston had brought the majority of his division by rail to reinforce Beauregard's heavily outnumbered Southern troops.

Although militarily the battle ended in deadlock it was in every other respect a Confederate victory. Stuart's "Black Horse" cavalry established their supremacy while the tenacity and discipline of Jackson's Virginians earned him the title "Stonewall." McDowell was forced to retire in disorder to the protection of Washington giving the South precious months in which to consolidate its defenses.

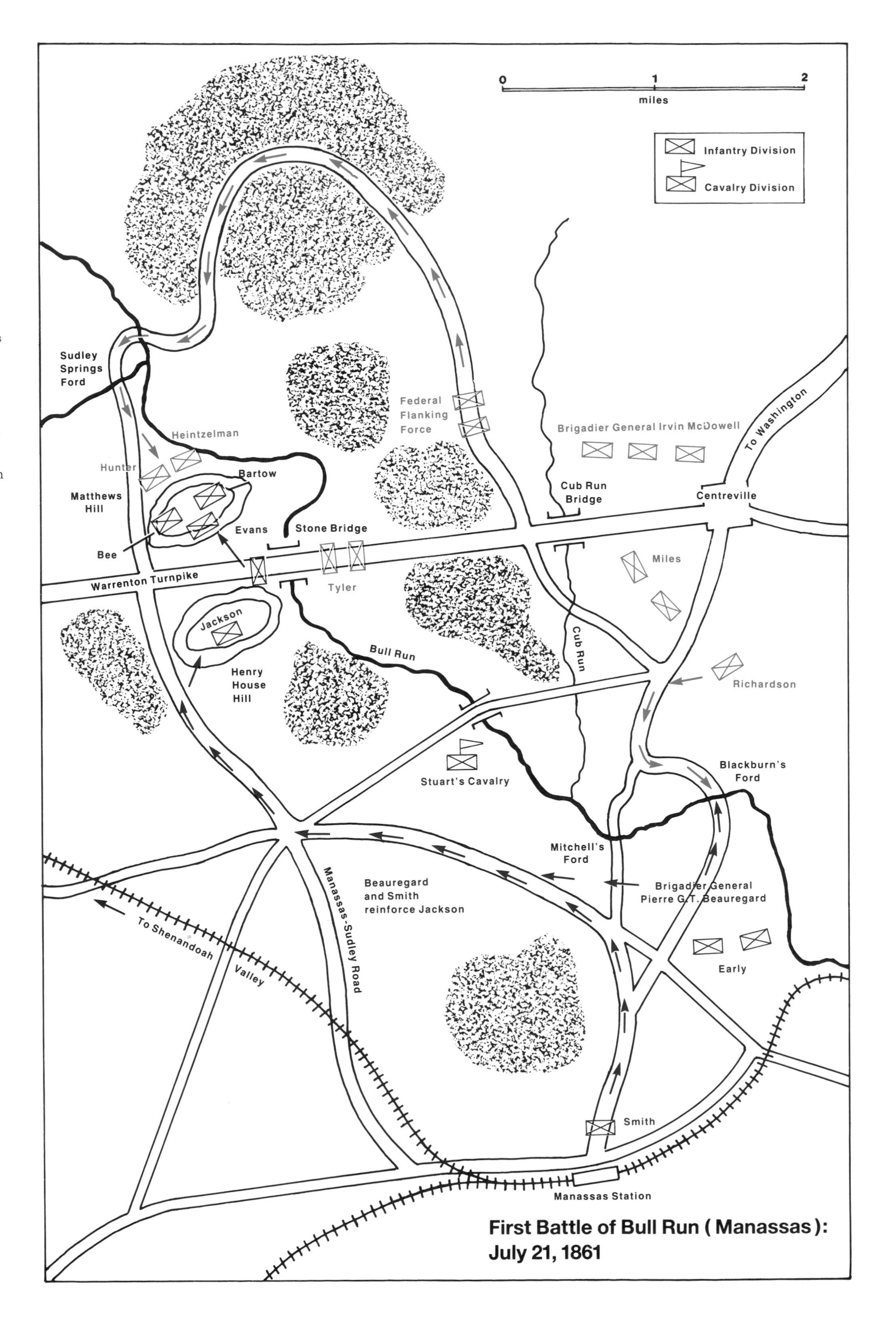

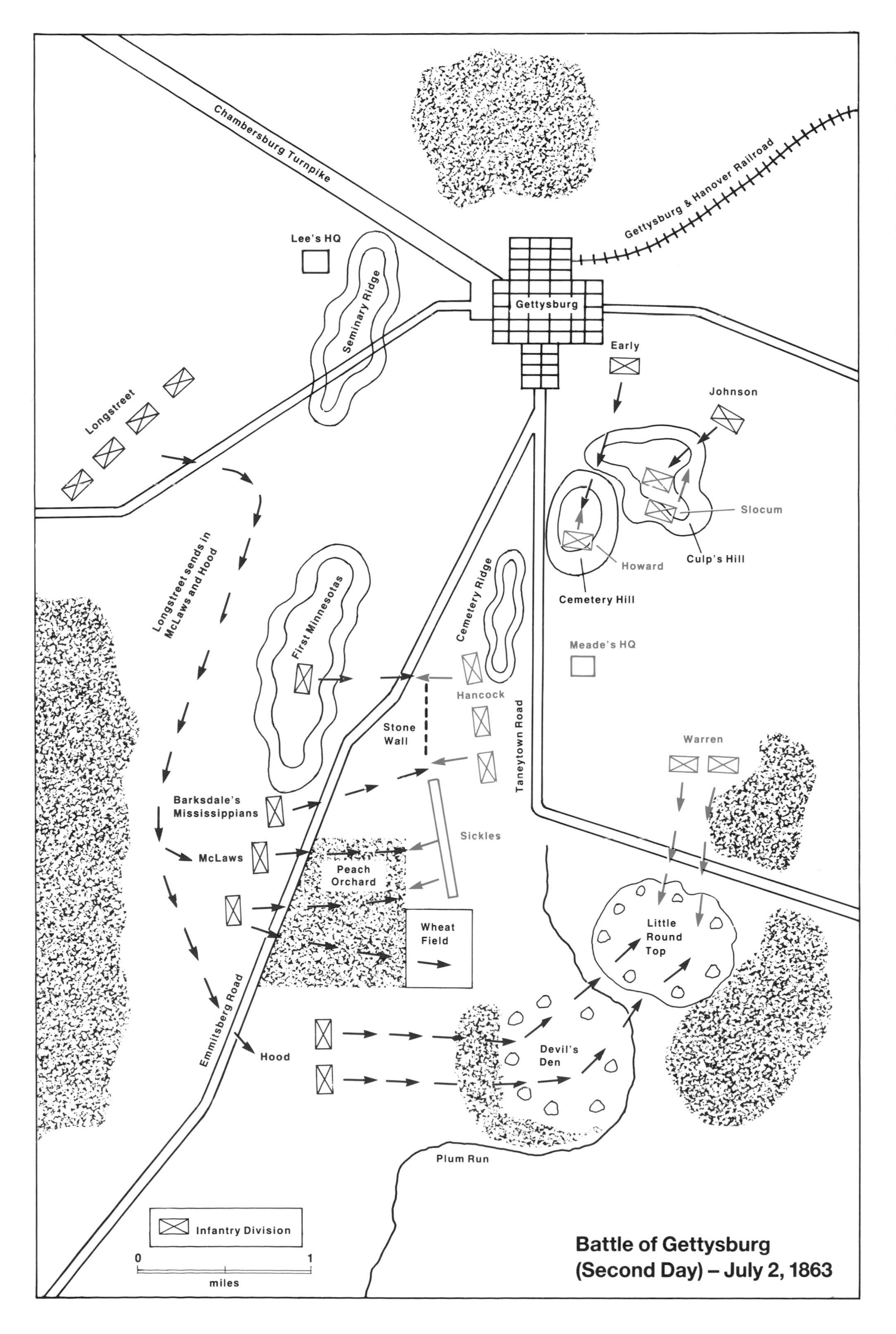

Gettysburg represented a desperate gamble on the part of the Confederacy. Determined to take the pressure off Virginia, Lee led his army into Pennsylvania to draw the Federal forces away from the South. Denied cavalry support by Stuart, who had inexplicably led his seasoned veterans on a lengthy unauthorized raid deep behind enemy lines, Lee was forced to join battle on Federal terms.

Gettysburg witnessed acts of extreme valor on the part of both armies particularly in the areas of Stone Wall and Little Round Top. After three days of vicious fighting Lee was forced to withdraw the remnants of his army south towards the protection of Virginia. After Gettysburg a Federal victory could only be a matter of time.

Index

Alabama Troops
  Irregular Cavalry 24
  38th Regiment 17
Alexander, E. P. 38
Ambulance train *13*
Ambulances 13
American Telegraph Company 38
Anaconda Plan 6
Andersonville Prison 53
Antietam Bridge *44*
Antietam (Sharpsburg), Battle of 14, 16, 17, 30, 33, 42
Appomattox 16, 26
Armstrong 600 pound gun *37*
Armstrong, William 37
Artillery, heavy 34–7, *35*
Atlanta, Battle for 46
Atlantic & Ohio Telegraph Company 38
Ayre's Division 30

Bachman, Lieutenant Colonel Alois 16
Balloon Corps 41
Banks' Command 17
Barry, Major William 34
Bartows' Brigade 20
Belle Isle Prison 53
Benton Barracks, Missouri 29
Bethesda Church 30
Birch Coulee, Battle of 29
Birney's Division 17
Bismarck, North Dakota 29
Black Hat Brigade (Iron Brigade of the West) *43*, 45
Black soldiers, Plymouth 52
Blanker, General, Bull Run *24*
Booth, Major Lionel 52
Brackett's Minnesota Cavalry 29
Brandy Station, Battle of 28
"Brooke" guns 37
Brown, Colonel William 16, 17
"Bucktails" (Pennsylvania 13th Reserves) 33
Bull Run
  1st Battle of Manassas 6, 20, 34, 42
  2nd Battle of Manassas 14, 16, 17, 30, 33, 42
Burnside, General Ambrose 25
Butterflies (1st U.S. Hussars) 28

U.S.S. *Cairo 8*
Cameron, Simon, Secretary for War 30
Camp Dennison 29
Camp Ford, Texas 53
Castle Pinckney Prison Camp *52, 53*
Casualties
  Chickamauga 10
  Iron Brigade of the West 45
  Marye's Heights *12*
  Pennsylvania 8th Reserves, 37th Volunteers 33
  19th Indiana Regiment 42, 44, 45
  20th Indiana Regiment 16, 17
Cavalry 26–9
  charge *26*
Cedar Mountain 17
Chalmers, Brigadier James 52
Chancellorsville, Battle of 17, 34, 42
Chaplains 46, *47*
Charleston, free port 8
chasseur field cap 9
Chattanooga 21
Chickamauga, casualties 10
Ciphers 41
Cloyd's Mountain 32
Coastal Defense guns 36
Cockeysville 16
Cold Harbor, Battle of 10, 12, 25, 30
Colgrove, Colonel Silas 17
Colt, revolver 39
Commissary Department 48
Comstock, Lieutenant Colonel 25
Confederate Bureau of War 52
Confederate Medical Department 10
Congress (ship) 9, 16
1st Connecticut Heavy Artillery 37
Contract Surgeons 10–12
Crater massacre 52
Crawford, General Samuel 30, 32
Crow's nest signal station *40*
Cumberland (ship) 9
Curtin, Governor Andrew 30
Custer, Colonel George 44

Dahlgren 11 inch cannons 9
"Dictator" 13-inch seige mortar 37
Disease 12
Dress Regulations, at sea *9*
DuPont, Flag Officer S. F. 6, 8

Electric telegraph 21
Ellendale, North Dakota 29
Elmira Prison NY 53
Enfield, P1853 14, 15
Ericsson, John 9

Farragut, Flag Officer David 6, 8
Federal Ambulance Corps 13
Federal Army, structure 23–5
Federal Military Telegraph System 38
Fisher's 3rd Brigade 30, 32
Fort Beauregard 8
Fort Berthold 29
Fort Donelson 16
Fort Fisher 6, *49*
Fort Halleck 29
Fort Jackson 8
Fort Laramie 29
Fort Mitchell 29
Fort Monroe 16
Fort Pickens 34
Fort Pillow massacre 52
Fort Rice 29
Fort Ridgley 29
Fort St. Philip 8
Fort Sumter 20, 30, *37*
Fort Walker 8
Fox, Gustavus 8
Fredericksburg 42
  Battle of *13*, 30, 33
  Campaign 25
Fuller, General 25

Gaine's Mill 33
Gettysburg
  Battle of 16, 30, 59
  Campaign 42
Gibbon, Brigadier John 42, 44
Glendale 17
Goldsborough 6
Gordon's 3rd Brigade 17
Grant, General 21, 32, 37, 41, 50
  dress 25
  personal staff 22–4
Grapeshot 36
Gregg, Captain (Chaplain) 48
Groveton 44
Gunner, heavy artillery 35

Haney, Rev Milton 46
"Hardee" hats 14, *15*
"Harpers Ferry", M1855 14, *17*
Hatch, John Porter 45
Hatch's New Yorkers 42, 45
Hatteras Inlet 6, 16
Haupt, Herman 20, *21*
Hospital Stewards *11*, 12–13, *13*
Hospitals 13
Howitzers 36
Humphreys' Division *33*
Humphreys, General Andrew 12, 24

Illinois Troops 26–8
  9th Infantry 28
  55th Infantry 46
  92nd Infantry 28
Indiana Troops 14–17
  attack on Fort Donelson *16–17*
  Gettysburg, Battle of 16, 17
  Iron Brigade of the West 14, 42
  Petersburg 16
  uniform 14, *14*, *15*
  volunteers 14
  Wilderness 16
  XII Corps 17
  1st Brigade 16
  1st-11th Regiments 14
  3rd Division, III Corps 16, 17
  17th Infantry 28
  19th Regiment 14, 42, 44, 45
  20th Regiment 16, 17
  27th Regiment 17
  72nd Infantry 28
Ingalls, Brevet Maj Gen. Rufus *22*
Iowa Troops 28
  6th Cavalry 29
  7th Cavalry 29
Iron Brigade of the West 14, 15, 42–5
  at Gettysburg *45*
  Bull Run *42*
  casualties 45
  uniforms *43*

Jackson, Thomas "Stonewall" 20, 33
Jackson's Campaign 17
James, Colonel 37

Kane, Colonel Thomas 30, 33
Kane County Rifles 33
Kearney, Major General 16
Killdeer 29
King, Rufus 42
Knoxville 20

Lances *27*
Landregan, Private James 33
Lee, General 8, 20, 30
Lewinsville, 14
Lincoln, President 6, 20, 24
  criticism 46
  exchange of prisoners 50
  retaliation 52

Lindley, John 14
Little Big Horn, Battle of 44
Lowe, Thaddeus 41

McCall, George Archibald 32
McCallum, Daniel Craig 20
McCandless' 1st Brigade 30, 32
McClellan, Gen. George Brinton 16, 34, 41
McClellan hat 27
McDowell, General 20
McDowell's I Corps 30
McKean, Flag Officer 6
Magilton's 2nd Brigade 30
Maine Regiments
  1st Heavy Artillery 37
  7th Infantry 28
Manassas (Bull Run)
  1st Battle of 6, 20, 34, 42, 58
  2nd Battle of 14, 16, 17, 30, 33, 42
Manassas Junction 20
Maps 54–59
Marye's Heights *12*, 33
Maryland Campaign 42
May, Major Isaac 16
Meade, Maj Gen. George 12, 24, 25, *25*, 32
Meade's V Corps 30
Meagher, Major General Thomas *14*
Medical Cadets 10–12
Meigs, Quartermaster General Montgomery C. 48
Meikel, Lieutenant Colonel 17
Mendell, Captain G. H. 25
Meredith, Solomon 14, 44
Merrimac (frigate) 9, 16
Mexican War 14
Michigan Regiments
  Iron Brigade of the West 42
  24th Regiment 42, 45
Military Telegraph 38, *41*
Military Telegraph Corps 41
Minnesota Troops
  Brackett's Minnesota Cavalry 29
  1st Mounted Rangers 29
  2nd Cavalry 29
Mississipi Marine Brigade 7, 9
Missouri Cavalry and Infantry 28
Model, 1842 musket 14, 15
Monitor (ship) 9
Monitor-Merrimac (Virginia) engagement 16
Morse Code 21, 38
Mortar Battery *36*
Mortars 36
  railroad trolley *18*
Morton, Governor 14
Mounted Infantry 28
Myer, Albert James 38

"Napoleons" 12 pounder guns 34, *34*
Nebraska Troops, 2nd Cavalry 29
New Jersey Troops, 3rd Cavalry 28
New Orleans, assault 8
New Ulm, seige 29
New York Herald 46
New York Troops 28
  Hatch's Iron Brigade 45
  New York Volunteers 45
  2nd U.S. Sharpshooters 45
  8th Heavy Artillery 37
  129th Infantry 37
Newspapers 46

Northern Virginia, Army of 30
Nurses, women 13

Ohio Sharpshooters 24
Ohio Troops 24, 29
Ordnance Board 49
Orr, Colonel William 16

Pay 48
Peninsula Campaign 16–17, 30, 41
Pennsylvania Railroad 20
Pennsylvania Troops
  Bucktails *30*
  Reserves 30–3, *31*
  Rifles 33
  1st Cavalry 30
  1st Light Artillery 30
  1st-13th Regiments 30–2
  1st-13th Reserves 30, 33
  6th Cavalry 27, 28
  8th Reserves 30, 33
  10th Reserves 30, 33
  11th Reserves 30, 33
  30th-42nd Volunteers 30
  114th Infantry *32*
  127th Volunteer Infantry 48
  190th Volunteers 30
  191st Volunteers 30
Petersburg 17, 37
Plaquemine Bend 8
Plymouth, North Carolina 52
Poison Spring massacre 52
Port Royal 6, 8
Porter, Commander 8
Porter, Lieutenant Colonel 25
Porter's V Corps 30
Potomac, Army of the 13, 14, 24, 25, 42
Prisoners of war 50–3, *50, 51, 52*

Quartermaster Bureau 48
Quartermaster Corps 13
Quartermasters Department 41

Rabbis 46
Railroad engineer, civilian *19*
Railroads, construction 18–21
Rations 49
Redwood Agency 29
Resaca 17
Reynolds, John Fulton 32
Robinson, Brigadier 16
Rodman, Captain Thomas 36
Rosecrans, William S. 21
Rush's Lancers (6th Pennsylvania Cavalry) 28

Scott, Gen. Winfield 6
Scott, Thomas 20
Seminary Ridge 42
Seven Days Campaign 20, 33
Seven Pines, Battle of *10*
Sharps carbine *29*
Shenandoah Valley 17
Sherman, General 13, 21, 24, 25
Signal Corps 38–41, *39*
Signalling 41
Sioux, war 29
South Mountain 14, 33
Spiritual Welfare, troops 46
Spotsylvania, Battle of 10, 17, 33
Staff Officers 22–5, *22, 23, 25*

Stager, Anson 38
Stanton, Edwin, Secretary of War 38
Stonewall Jackson's Virginians *30*
Store-keepers (suttlers) 48
Stuart, Jeb 26
Sully, General Alfred 29
Supply column *48–9*
Supply train *46*
Support troops 46–9, *47*
Sweetwater Station 29
Sykes' V Corps 30

Taylor, Colonel William 16
Texas, secession 26
Topographical Engineers 41
Trains *see* railroads

United States Military Railway Service 20
U.S. Army Medical Department 10
U.S. Army Troops
Cavalry Regiments *27*
1st U.S. Cavalry 26, *28*
4th U.S. Artillery 42
5th U. S. Artillery 34
U.S. Marine Corps 6–9, *6,* 7
U.S. Military Railroad Engineers 18–21
U.S. Ordnance Board 49
U.S. Secretary of the Interior 20
U.S. Signal Corps 38–41

Veteran Reserve Brigade 30
Veteran Reserve Corps 46
Vicksburg 8
Vicksburg Incident 50
Virginia (ship) 8, 9
Volunteer Cavalry 26–9, *27, 28*

Wahpeton Sioux, Minnesota 29
Wallace, Colonel-in-chief Lew 14
Ward's Brigade 17
Warren, Major General 25
West Virginia, Army of 32
Western Union Telegraph Company 38
Wheeler, Colonel John 16, 17
Whitestone Hill, Battle of 29
Wigwag System 38
Wilderness Campaign 10, 17, 32, 33, 37
Williams' 1st Division 17
Williams, Colonel Samuel 14, 16
Wilmington, free port 7
Wirz, Henry 53
Wisconsin Troops
  Iron Brigade of the West 42
  uniforms 44–5
  2nd Regiment 42, 44, 45
  6th Regiment 42, 44, 45
  7th Regiment 42
Wood Lake, Battle of 29

Yellow Tavern, Battle of 28

Zouaves 14, *53*

Acknowledgements
4 volume set (originally published as Combat Uniforms of the Civil War)

Alabama Department of Archives and History, Hulton Getty, Library of Congress, Museum of the Confederacy, National Archives, North Carolina State Division of Archives, Peter Newark's Western Americana, Smithsonian Institution, Texas State Library, Virginia Military Institute.